The
Successful
Investor

The
Successful
Investor

What 80 Million People
Need to Know
to Invest Profitably
and Avoid Big Losses

William J. O'Neil

McGraw-Hill

New York   Chicago   San Francisco   Lisbon   London   Madrid
Mexico City   Milan   New Delhi   San Juan   Seoul
Singapore   Sydney   Toronto

1 2 3 4 5 6 7 8 9 0   DOC/DOC   0 9 8 7 6 5 4 3

ISBN 0-070-142959-X

Printed and bound by RR Donnelley.

Contents

Foreword   *vii*

Introduction   *ix*

A Word About Charts   *xvii*

Step 1 Which Way Is the General Market Going?   1

Step 2 Use a Simple 3-to-1 Profit-and-Loss Percentage Plan   17

Step 3 How to Buy the Very Best Stocks
        at the Very Best Time   35

Step 4 When to Sell and Nail Down Your Big Profit
        While You Still Have It   75

Step 5 Managing Your Portfolio: Time-Proven Methods
        to Maximize Results and Minimize Losses   96

Appendix A *How to Use the CAN SLIM Approach*
              to Screen for Growth Stocks   *141*

Appendix B *All About CAN SLIM*   *155*

Appendix C *Market Memo*   *161*

Appendix D *Testimonials for* The Successful Investor   *163*

Appendix E *A Loud Warning to the Wise*
              About Bear Markets!!!   *173*

Index   *175*

Foreword

After three years of an extremely difficult stock market that began in March 2000, where most investors lost more than they needed to, I realized that every investor—new or supposedly experienced—needed much more investment knowledge and realistic help.

So, I decided to get this book out ASAP to help the millions of investors in the sure market recovery and future rewarding, yet confusing, markets that always have and always will occur. I outlined all the vital subjects, crucial methods, techniques, and key points that investors must learn if they want to be highly successful investors.

I then enlisted Wes Mann, IBD's very fine editor and a successful investor in his own right, to help. We turned on his tape recorder and I talked my way through the whole book, point by point, with Wes asking clarification questions on subjects that might not be easily understood by everyone. The recording was typed, word for word. I edited it; Wes edited it and polished all of the awkward sentences, being careful not to change meanings. Next, I picked all the chart examples and marked on each the important elements all investors need to understand if they want to know how to read charts. Charts can help improve your selection of the best stocks and timing of both buy and sell decisions in stocks, as well as the general market. (Lack of sell rules and the ability to spot major selling indicators in a stock's price and trading volume action, and in general market indexes, constitute one key reason so many people lost so much more than they should have.)

Additionally, many thanks must go out to the following people who also contributed their time and effort to the completion of *The Successful Investor*: Philip Ruppel and his excellent professional staff at McGraw-Hill, Justin Nielsen, Deirdre Abbott, Sharon Brooks, Gary Flam, Angela Han, Gil Morales, Wendy Reidt, and Mike Webster.

Introduction

Why this book now? If you're a stock or mutual fund investor, you probably already know the answer. Chances are you're one of the 80 million Americans who lost 50 to 80 percent of your hard-earned life savings in the market decline that began in the spring of 2000. And you never, ever want that to happen again. But unless you make it a point to learn what happened to you—what went wrong and why—there's no guarantee that history won't repeat itself.

The purpose of this book is to help you see some of the mistakes you made and could make again unless you adopt sound rules and principles to guide your future investment decisions. Only then will you be on the road to the kind of investment results that can and will materially improve your life. And if you're a new investor, you certainly want to learn what not to do as well as what to do to become a successful investor.

But, you say, wasn't the recent market debacle a once-in-a-lifetime event? Well, yes and no. The market bubble that formed in the anything-goes 1990s and blew up in the early 2000s was unusual. We hadn't seen anything like it in 70 years. But it was different only in degree. If measured by the NASDAQ, home to most of the high-tech stocks that got so inflated, the 1990s market went up even more than the superheated bull run of the Roaring Twenties. And the losses that followed rivaled those suffered in the Crash of 1929 that led to the Great Depression.

The wild market of the 1990s can even be equated with the tulip bulb mania of 1636. Everyone then believed the whole world would have to buy tulip bulbs from Holland. As a result, prices of bulbs

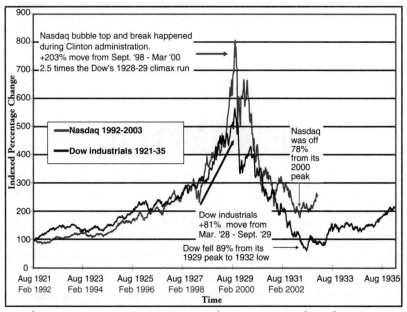

Nasdaq Composite 1992–2003 Compared to Dow Jones Industrials 1921–1935

traded on the Dutch stock exchange reached astronomical heights before they came crashing down to earth. It was much the same with the Internet craze of the 1990s, when investors had to own a piece of every company with "dot-com" attached to its name.

Otherwise, the latest market cycle was much like all those that preceded it. I know. I've been in the market day in and day out, through every bull and bear cycle, for the last 45 years—both as an individual investor and as an advisor to many of the best investment managers in the country. Moreover, as the head of a top database research firm, I've also conducted one of the most definitive studies ever done of the market and the stocks that always lead it.

What impresses me most—even after going through a period like 1998 to 2002—is how little things change. The losses suffered in the most recent decline may have been extraordinary, but the mistakes that led to them were not. They were the same mistakes investors have made in every cycle.

When you think about it, the reason for this becomes obvious. The market is made up of millions of people acting almost 100 percent on human emotion and personal opinion. It is crowd psychology on daily display. And—especially when it comes to the hopes and fears and pride and ego that drive so many investment decisions—human nature is pretty much the same now as it was in 1929 or 1636.

What you must understand, though, is that highly successful investing has nothing to do with your emotions or personal opinions. The stock market doesn't care who we as individuals are, what we think, or how we feel. It's a beast like no other: indifferent to human desires, oblivious to common wisdom, maddeningly contrary, and seemingly bent on confounding the majority at every turn. The only law it obeys is the law of supply and demand. And until you, as an investor, come to grips with this reality and learn to move with the market rather than against it, you'll be plagued by results that are mediocre at best.

This would be a shame considering that Americans are taking more responsibility for their financial well-being. It won't be long, for example, until the Social Security system will be at least partially privatized. Then you'll be able to take some of the money that the government sets aside for your later years (and has invested for a pathetic return) and invest it yourself.

Deferring to the market's opinion instead of your own won't be easy. And the smarter you are, the more difficult it may be. You may be highly educated with advanced degrees and accomplished in your own line of work. You may in fact be an expert whose opinion on the things you know most about usually goes unchallenged. But that can make it hard for you to see or admit it when you're wrong on an investment decision into which you've put so much time, thought, and ego. In the market, who you are and what you think mean nothing. Repeat: nothing. The market's going to do whatever it's going to do. And arguing with it can only cost you money.

Some of the biggest mistakes I saw in the 1998 to 2002 market were made by some of smartest people I've met. I remember a Ph.D. with a high-level management position telling me he bought Cisco Systems, one of the best-performing stocks of the 1990s, when it dropped to $50 because it was such a great company. I just hope he swallowed his pride of opinion and got out before that great company got down to $8.

Nor are professional investors immune from making amateurish mistakes. A bond fund manager I know bought WorldCom at $1.50, believing it simply couldn't get any cheaper after falling all the way from $64. Well, it could and did, changing hands at 17 cents the last time I looked.

Most people, both investors and advisors, got hurt in the 2000 to 2002 downturn because they never took the time to learn sound investment rules and principles. In the '90s they thought they'd found a way to make money without doing much homework. They just bought tips, touts, and stories.

They didn't grasp the realities of market risk or how to guard against major losses. They didn't have a way of telling if the market was headed up or turning down. And worst of all, they didn't have any sell rules!

But what the heck: life was good and everything seemed so easy. We got careless and carried away. Even some corporate leaders thought it was OK to lie, cheat, and exaggerate. After all, the leader of the country did, and it didn't seem to hurt him.

In the stock market, all you had to do was buy high-techs on every dip, because they always came back and increased in price. Opinions, however naive, were plentiful. So were experts, most of whom kept popping up on all-day TV market shows telling us what to buy. Friends, neighbors, advisors, salespeople—all stood ready to offer their own advice, whether we wanted it or not. And all seemed able to back it up with investment theories, however flaky.

For many, playing the market got to be just that: a sport or national pastime in which nearly everyone participated. At the gym where I work out, I remember a couple of fellows pooh-poohing Yahoo!, the Internet search engine, when it was in the early stages of its 100-fold move. A couple of years later, I overheard two others pumping iron and proclaiming all you needed to do to make a lot of money was buy Yahoo! every time it corrected, or pulled back in price. It was apparent to me that they had missed Yahoo! on most of its way up in the late 1990s. Now it had become an obvious sure thing to the crowd at the gym. The stock plunged from $250 a share in January 2000 to $8 by September 2001. The guys at the gym don't talk much about the market anymore.

When the bubble burst in March 2000, hardly anyone (except *Investor's Business Daily®*, the national financial newspaper we started in 1984) gave consistent sell advice or repeated warnings to reduce exposure and raise cash. Investors were left to learn the hard way a basic market truth: personal opinions, feelings, hopes, and beliefs about the stock market are usually wrong and often dangerous. Facts and markets, on the other hand, are seldom wrong. The law of supply and demand works better than all the opinions of all the analysts on Wall Street or off.

Most investors now realize they need to know much more about what they're doing when they invest their hard-earned money. They know they need sound, time-tested rules and procedures to make real profits while at the same time protecting themselves from serious losses. Isn't it about time you got serious about your money and investments by reading, learning, reevaluating, and significantly improving your methods?

When I started investing, I made most of the same mistakes you've probably made. I know how bad habits are formed and how hard it is to break them. But break them you must, so you can develop new habits based on how the market actually works. These new habits may seem strange at first. They'll force you to do things that you and most people don't like to do, are not used to doing, or never understood you should do. But they will, if correctly applied over time, produce a dramatic improvement in your investment performance. For example:

- You buy stocks on the way up in price, not on the way down. And when you buy more, you do it after the stock has risen from your purchase price, not after it's fallen below it.
- You buy stocks nearer their highs for the year, not when they've sunk so low they look cheap. You buy higher-priced stocks rather than the lowest-priced stocks.
- You learn to always sell stocks quickly when you have a small loss rather than waiting and hoping they'll come back.
- You pay far less attention to a company's book value, dividends, or PE ratio—which for the last 50 years have had little predictive value in spotting America's most successful companies—and

focus instead on more important proven factors such as profit growth, price and volume action, and if the company is the number 1 profit leader in its field.

- You don't subscribe to a bunch of market newsletters or advisory services, and you don't let yourself be influenced by recommendations from analysts who, again, are just expressing personal opinions that can be frequently wrong.

You also have to acquaint yourself with charts—an invaluable tool that most professionals wouldn't do without but that amateurs tend too dismiss as complicated or irrelevant.

To significantly improve my own investment results, I did three things. First, I studied only what the very best people with the very best performance records did in their own market decision making. These include Jack Dreyfus of the mutual fund organization that bears his name, in the late 1950s; Fidelity Investments' Ned Johnson and Jerry Tsai, in the early 1960s; Gerald Loeb, a stock broker and author of *The Battle for Investment Survival,* who made money from the 1920s through the 1960s; and Jesse Livermore, whose markets exploits and methods were covered in fascinating detail in Edwin Lefevre's 1923 classic, *Reminiscences of a Stock Operator.* All these professionals produced far superior results at certain periods in their careers.

Second, after I made mistakes and lost money or gave back most of my profits, I plotted on weekly charts exactly where I had bought and sold each stock. I analyzed what I did wrong when I lost money or blew a great opportunity. Then I designed and wrote down new rules that I carefully followed to prevent the same mistakes from happening again. These rules were written on one or two pages at the front of a little zipper notebook I kept with me every market day.

Third, I cut out and collected about 50 charts of the top-performing stocks from several prior years. I wanted to know how they looked both fundamentally (earnings growth, etc.) and technically (price and volume action) before they doubled or tripled in price. I then noted what key characteristics they all had in common, so I knew what factors to look for in the future.

How well has all of this worked out? What kind of actual result has it produced? From 1998 through 2002, the American Association of Individual Investors (AAII) conducted its own real-time month-to-month study and analysis of our system, which we call CAN SLIM™ Investment Research Tools (see Appendix B). AAII, a Chicago-based organization, compared the results of our system and rules as defined and explained in my earlier book, *How to Make Money in Stocks,* with the performance of 52 other widely known investment systems, including those of Peter Lynch and Warren Buffett.

According to AAII's April 2003 journal article by John Bajkowski (see Appendix A):

> . . . AAII has been testing the performance of a wide range of screening systems for over five years, and our interpretation of the CAN SLIM approach has been one of the most consistent and strongest performing screens during both bull and bear markets.

AAII's independent research results found CAN SLIM's performance to be as follows: 1998, +28.2 percent; 1999, +36.6 percent; 2000, +38.0 percent; 2001, +54.4 percent; 2002, +20.7 percent, for a total five-year compounded return of +350.3 percent during two bull market (up) years and three extremely difficult bear market (down) years. Over the same five year period, the S&P 500 was down 8.3 percent. Out of approximately 10,000 equities screened by AAII on March 14, 2003 according to our rules, only four stocks survived AAII's screening. They were Apollo (APOL) $47.84, which by June 30 closed at $61.80; FTI Consulting (FCN) $28.30, closing June at $24.97; International Game Technology (IGT) $78.01, closing June at $102.33; and Teva Pharmaceutical (TEVA) $38.10, closing June at $56.90. The average increase was 24.5 percent.

During the 1980s and 1990s, thousands of dedicated, motivated subscribers to *Investor's Business Daily* who studied and applied all our rules and methods made net gains of several hundred percent to 1000 percent or more. Many joined the ranks of millionaires. Not everyone, of course, found it easy to cut all losses quickly, as we preached repeatedly, or to follow our rules on when to sell and nail down worthwhile gains. Just skimming our material, or not executing with real discipline and determination, or not understanding the rules of how to recognize a market top, assuredly produced a much more disappointing result.

Our internal money management group operating from our Data Analysis holding company produced a 1356 percent net return in the five-year period ending June 2003.

Readers who closely followed and understood the daily factual analysis of general market action in IBD's "Big Picture" column, as well as the hundreds of educational articles in "Investor's Corner," sold stocks and raised cash in March and April of 2000.

An even longer period of real-time performance applying our CAN SLIM investment system is the "New Stock Market Ideas" (NSMI) book published weekly for institutional investors by our sister firm, William O'Neil + Co., since 1977. From that time to the end of 2002, the NSMI service chalked up a total return of 26,173 percent. Compounding results each year makes such a mind-boggling result possible. It was over 6 times the result achieved during the same time period by Value Line's excellent-performing number-one-ranked stocks and compared to a gain in the S&P 500 of 909 percent.

The real secret to why our system has worked so well for thousands of serious, dedicated investors is that it's not based on my personal views, beliefs, or opinions. CAN SLIM is based 100 percent on the facts learned from our comprehensive study of every outstanding stock performer each year for the past half century. All the traits they shared prior to their periods of greatest performance became our buy rules. And how the variables changed when each big leader finally topped became our sell rules.

So when you violate any of the rules and principles we will disclose to you in this book, you will probably make many more unwanted mistakes. You will be arguing with how the stock market has in reality worked for many, many years.

Added to our meticulous analysis of historical models is years of experience working with and providing research ideas to many of the best institutional investors in the U.S. We built the first daily historical stock market database in 1963, and today William O'Neil + Co. has more than 600 of the world's largest institutional investors as regular clients of our computerized research, one example of which is the WONDA® service, a powerful interface with our database.

We had none of the problems faced by some Wall Street firms in 2002 because our business is completely different and independent.

We publish no fundamental analyst research reports or recommendations, do no investment banking, make no markets in securities, have no retail sales staff or retail branch offices dealing with the public, and do not deal in bonds, commodities, or currencies. We only do a highly specialized institutional business utilizing our own sophisticated and advanced historical computer database.

In this short book, I've boiled down the age-old secrets of how you can become the successful investor to just five simple steps. If you have the desire and determination to read and reread these steps many times until you become skillful in understanding and applying each of them, your investment results should improve to the point you'll be able to afford a much better life and more of the things you want. It doesn't take a lot of money or an Ivy League education. Anyone can do it. You can do it. So go for it. It's all up to you.

A Word About Charts

A picture, they say, is worth a thousand words. But to the successful investor, a picture in the form of a stock chart is worth a lot more. And not just in words. Like the x-rays used by doctors, charts tell you at a knowledgeable glance if an individual stock, or the stock market in general, is healthy or sick. In so doing, they let you know if you should be in or out of the stock or in or out of the market. And that, as you will see, makes all the difference.

If you're not familiar with charts, or think they're too technical, don't worry. You were probably afraid of the water the first time you were taken to a swimming pool. But given a little time, and perhaps a few swimming lessons, they couldn't get you out of the pool.

You might not take to charts with the same alacrity. But you'll find that, with a little effort, understanding the patterns that charts sketch out will dramatically improve your future investment results.

The more time you spend with charts, moreover, the more skilled you'll become. You will not only be able to recognize patterns that presage enormous stock moves, you'll also be able to detect patterns that are absolutely defective and must be avoided. This is of enormous value in helping cut down on your costly mistakes.

Many cynics, because of their lack of knowledge, put chart reading in the same category as reading tea leaves. But they haven't stopped to think how professionals in most walks of life use charts to make better decisions. No doctor, for example, would feel confident in making a diagnosis of your physical condition without that x-ray or EKG or MRI.

Professionals in the world of investing use charts the same way. And the most successful ones would no more buy or sell a stock before looking at its chart than a doctor would treat you without looking at the images he or she has to work with.

The figure below shows a bar chart—the type most commonly used by investors. It's drawn in two dimensions: price and time. The price scale runs up and down the right side; the time scale runs along the bottom. In this case, the interval is one week. In other words, each bar represents a week's price action in terms of three measurements. The top of the bar marks the highest price the stock traded that week. The bottom of the bar marks the low for the period. The crosshatch, or horizontal tick mark, shows the stock's close, or last price that week.

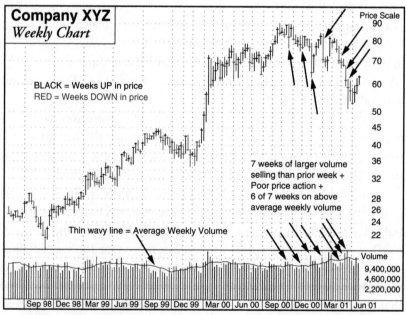

Weekly Chart Has Seven Weeks of Volume Selling. . . . Sell the Stock!

At the very bottom of the chart are bars that serve as thermometers measuring the stock's weekly trading volume.

This chart, for example, shows that on the last week of trading, shown at the far right, the stock's price got as high as about $64, almost got as low as $60, and closed at $63½, near its peak for the week. Volume totaled well over 10 million shares. The week before, its high was about $63, its low was just over 56½, and the close for the week was slightly below $60. Volume for those five days increased to over 20 million shares.

Up weeks (when the stock closes higher than it did the previous week) are shown in black and down weeks (when it closes lower) are shown in red, just to make it easier for you to see the difference. This will come in handy, as you'll see later.

You may notice that the price scale looks a little funny. In certain parts it's stretched out; in others it's compressed, kind of like an accordion. The reason is that this chart has been plotted logarithmically rather than arithmetically. I prefer log charts because they show stock or market moves in the right proportion. In other words, the 100 percent rise in a stock that goes from 40 to 80 is shown to be twice as steep on the chart as the 50 percent gain when it continues from 80 to 120, even though both moves amount to 40 points.

You will find more charts like this, with markings just like those I've made here, throughout this book. As we go, we'll be adding more lines that impart even more information. By the end, you'll know how to use all of them to tell you things that 99 percent of other investors will never see, let alone act on. In other words, you'll be investing like a pro.

Now that we've walked you through it, the basic chart may look pretty simple. Does it tell a story? You bet. From just these few lines, I can see that here is a stock that's done well for a long time and would have been well worth owning. But now I can see that it's getting into trouble—that the many buyers who've been bidding it up and up and up for so long are now getting overwhelmed by sellers. There's no way I would consider buying this stock, no matter how well it's done in the past, how well the company seems to be doing in the present, or how cheap it may seem because it's down in price. And if I owned it, I'd be thinking hard about selling it.

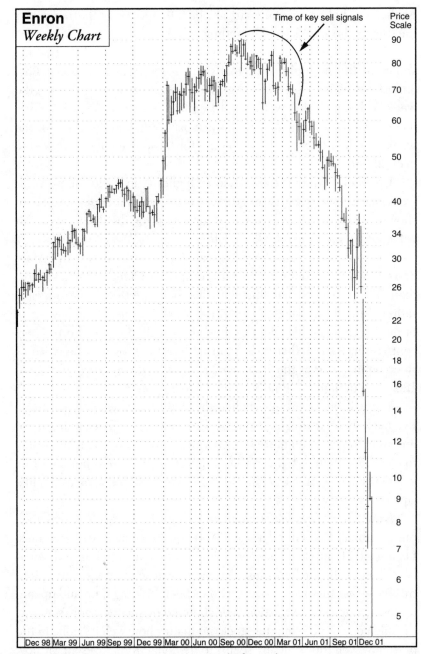

Enron's Top and Aftermath

In fact, the chart shows how Enron Corp. looked in April 2001, just before it plunged more than 99 percent and eventually went bankrupt, causing untold heartbreak for its thousands of employees and shareholders and giving our economic system a black eye that has yet to heal. If only they had known how to use charts and to recognize the tragedy that was unfolding before their very eyes!

Yes, this is a short book. But if each picture is worth 1000 words, you can add a million more.

STEP 1

Which Way Is the General Market Going

Why start here—with directions on how to tell if the stock market as a whole is going up or coming down? Because when the general market—as defined by the S&P 500 index, the NASDAQ composite index, and the Dow Jones industrial average—tops and turns down, three out of four of your stocks, regardless of their quality or how they're performing, will go down too.

Besides, if you learn to recognize when the market is topping, you'll have a skill that very few investors have developed. And that includes pros on Wall Street. As a group, they failed to tell their customers to sell stock and raise cash in 2000, when the whole market was topping and 98 percent of all individual investors got hurt.

What did the brokers, strategists, and economists do wrong? They relied purely on their own opinions of what the market would do. They also relied too much on their interpretation of the dozens of business and economic indicators they favor.

This approach rarely if ever works because the economy does not lead the market, the market leads the economy. That's why wiser souls years ago included the S&P 500 index, a proxy for the general market, as one of the "leading" economic indicators released by the government each month and not a "coincidental" or "lagging" indicator. In

1

short, the experts on Wall Street, by using the economy as a predictor of the stock market rather than vice versa, had it all backward.

Another group of experts, called market technicians, follows 50 to 100 technical indicators such as advance-decline lines, sentiment gauges, and overbought-oversold measures. But in 45 years, I can't recall a technician picking both a market top and the eventual market bottom. At best, they're usually right one time and wrong the next. The reason is that the vast array of technical indicators they follow are secondary and far less accurate than the general market averages.

There's an important lesson here. To be highly accurate in any pursuit, you must carefully observe and analyze the object itself. If you want to know about tigers, watch tigers—not the weather, not the vegetation, not the other animals on the mountain.

Years ago, when Lou Brock set his mind to breaking baseball's stolen base record, he had all the big-league pitchers photographed with high-speed film from the seats behind first base. Then he studied the film to learn what part of each pitcher's body moved first when he threw to first base. The pitcher was the object Brock was trying to beat, so it was the pitchers themselves he studied in great detail.

In the 2003 Super Bowl, the Tampa Bay Buccaneers were able to intercept five Oakland Raider passes by first studying and then concentrating on the eye movements and body language of Oakland's quarterback. They "read" where he was going to throw.

Christopher Columbus didn't accept the conventional wisdom about the earth being flat because he himself had observed ships at sea disappearing over the horizon in a way that told him otherwise. The government uses wiretaps, spy planes, unmanned drones, and satellite photos to observe and analyze the objects that could threaten our security. That's how we discovered Soviet missiles in Cuba.

It's the same with the stock market. To know which way it's going, you must observe and analyze the major general market indexes daily. Don't ever, ever ask anyone: "What do you think the market's going to do?" Learn to accurately read what the market is actually doing daily as it is doing it.

When the market is in an uptrend, advancing day by day, week by week, you want to follow not only the price action of the market averages each day but more importantly the daily volume. What you're observing is whether the total trading volume has increased or decreased from the day before. You're also taking note of whether that day's volume is above or below the recent average daily volume. What you want to see in an uptrending market is prices and trading volume rising in tandem for the most part. That shows a market under *accumulation,* with more buying than selling.

The easiest way to track this action is with the use of charts that show the high, low, and closing prices of the various indexes with volume plotted underneath. A proper chart will have the volume close enough to the price so you can easily move your eyes from one to the other, connecting the right day's price with the right day's volume.

In any uptrend, there will come a point when selling activity overtakes buying. This we call *distribution,* and it's important that you recognize it as it's happening. The first day of distribution is when the index closes down from the day before but on volume that is higher.

No uptrending market, however, is turned down by just one day of increased volume selling. What we've found, by studying every market top going back 50 years, is that three to five days (in recent years it's been five days) of volume distribution over a span of two to four weeks is sufficient to turn the market's uptrend into a downtrend.

What you're watching for, then, after an initial day of distribution, is a second, then a third, fourth, and fifth. After the first day, the market may go up for two or three days before you see a second day when the market closes down with volume picking up. Around the second or third day, you start to get suspicious. By then, you've witnessed more selling than you'd like to see and you may have already sold a stock or two. By the fifth day, you realize the probability is extremely high that the entire market's rolling over and headed down.

There's another way the market signals distribution. We call it *stalling* action. In this case, the market will be moving higher in active trading and then suddenly have trouble making much further progress. It doesn't go down; it just doesn't go up much at all compared to the previous day or two. An example would be a market that has a clear uptrend for a number of weeks but then gains 40 points on heavy volume one day and the next day runs up as much as 30 or 40 but closes ahead only a point or two with trading the same as or heavier than on the prior day.

What's occurring in both situations is that something is suddenly stopping what has to that point been a relatively steady advance. That something is a change in the ratio of buying to selling. In an uptrending market, buying prevails. But when a market stalls on volume and starts heading down, it shows that increased selling has taken over.

Notice I don't say sellers. It isn't necessary that buyers outnumber sellers in an uptrending market. Accumulation can take place with more sellers than buyers if the buyers—large institutions such as mutual funds, for example—buy in larger quantities than the sellers sell. You can also have hundreds of people buying in small amounts who are easily overwhelmed by a handful of big institutions selling in quantity.

This is why it's so important to track both price and volume. If the market goes down but volume is less, it doesn't mean anything. But if volume picks up significantly, the numbers are telling a different story. They're saying that the supply-demand ratio is shifting to the point where the selling is increasing in intensity and having its effect.

In counting the three to five days of distribution, then, most of the days will actually be down and only one or maybe two might show little upside change. It's much easier to see the former. But the key is that you recognize and correctly count the volume distribution days in whatever form they take.

The distribution can occur on any one of the major indexes—the S&P 500, the NASDAQ composite, or the Dow industrials. On most days, *Investor's Business Daily* stacks charts of all three together on the same page, and I personally check each one in IBD™ each day. That way, I'm never asleep at the switch when the market comes under heavy distribution. If most stockbrokers and advisors learned this method of market analysis, they could save their clientele future disappointments and at the same time materially increase their business and client retention.

For further proof that a market is topping, you can also check the individual stocks that have led the advance. Our studies of market history show that these leaders top at the same time the distribution days are occurring. In a later chapter, we'll give you some valuable rules on when to sell stocks while they're still advancing and showing profits. You'll find that many of those rules will be tripped off at the very same

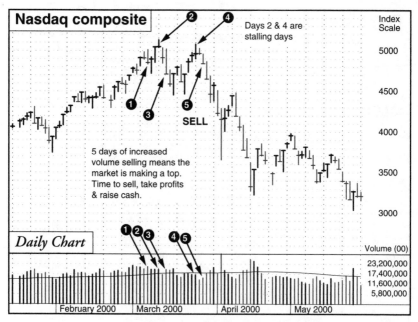

How the Stock Market Topped in March 2000

time the general market is coming under distribution. So now you have two different ways—the market indexes and the individual stock leaders—telling you when the market's starting to get into trouble.

At such points, you must be backing away and not making any purchases. You also want to be selling to raise some cash and definitely getting off margin, or using borrowed money. You want to stay in phase with what the market is actually doing, not with what you hope it will do or what other people think it should do. That's how 99 percent of the investing public operates. They're guided by personal opinions and their own and other people's guesses or hopes. You want facts—facts that tell you if the market is or isn't under significant distribution.

Your objective is to agree 100 percent with what is actually happening in the market rather than try to tell it what you think it ought to be doing. The market doesn't care who you are or what you think, hope, or want. Once you learn to recognize reality—what is actually occurring while it's occurring—you've acquired a skill and developed an awareness most people will never have. Even more important,

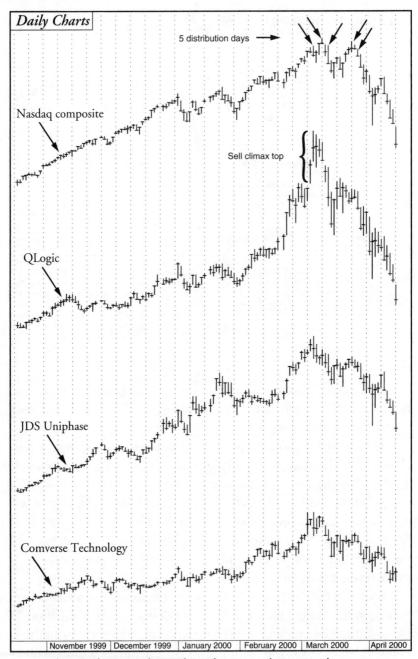

Leading Stocks Top as the Market Index Tops with Five Distribution Days

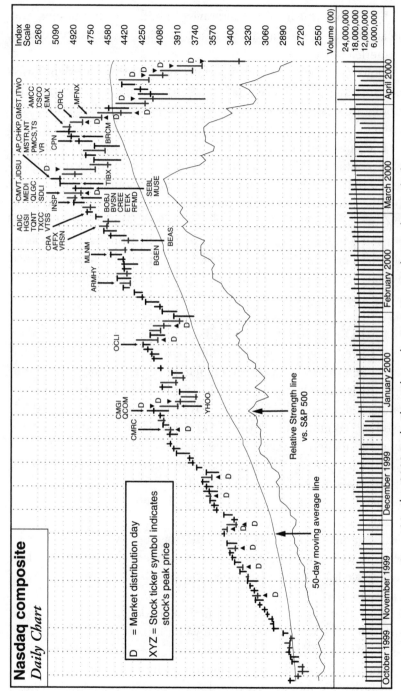

Nasdaq 2000 Daily Chart Shows the Days Key Market Leaders Peaked

you'll be selling, raising cash, and saving significant sums of money at crucial junctures, such as the 2000 top that just about every investor in America missed.

Don't get discouraged if you don't pick up this skill right away. Like anything else, it takes patience and practice. And during the learning process, you will sometimes misinterpret a distribution day or two.

The most common mistake I've seen involves a number of more tightly contained days where the index price spread from the high to the low of the day is very small and the actual amount of price decline from the prior day is also very small. So even though there is a volume increase and the price closes down, the movement is minor. If most of your three to five days are like this, the distribution may not be large enough to cause the market to turn down. Normally, however, down days on higher volume will be easy to spot, and the spreads between the high and low price for the day will be average to a little wider than average.

In IBD's new front-page "Big Picture" column, distribution days are observed, counted, and frequently pointed out with arrows on the market index charts on the general market page. Reading this column regularly is another way to refine and significantly improve your general market analytical skills. Many IBD subscribers who read and followed the column daily during 2000 were able to sell and raise cash when the column repeatedly explained the continuing distribution that was happening. This was worth an enormous fortune to those serious investors who paid close attention.

One last clue: bear markets frequently open higher at the beginning of the day's trading but then close down. Bull markets, in contrast, can open lower and close the day up. Also, if you notice lower-priced, lower-quality laggard stocks near the top of the daily most active list for several sessions, that may be a sign of a weakening general market.

Now that we've shown you how a market's major downtrend starts, let's turn to how you can tell when it ends and a new uptrend has begun—in other words, how you recognize a market bottom.

You never know how far a downtrending market will go. All you know is that it's under heavy distribution and it's going down. (Which is something most other people don't know at all, so you already have a huge edge.) Even though you don't know how far down the general market will go, you watch it day by day as it's declining. At some point, it will rally and recover for a few days. Pay no attention to the first and second days of the rally. There will always be upward blips in any general decline, but the major trend will still be down.

The only time in an attempted rally that you can conclude with greater reliability that the trend has changed from down to up is typically from the fourth day on. If the volume suddenly picks up from the day before with one or more of the major indexes posting a significant increase, you have what we call a confirmation of the rally that began with the first day up.

This confirmation, or follow-through, usually comes on the fourth through seventh days of an attempted rally. Sometimes it can come on the tenth day or even later and still be constructive, but rallies that follow through that late may not be as powerful. On the confirmation day, one key market index must be up a powerful and decisive amount, usually about 1.7 percent or more, on trading volume that's higher than the day before and typically better than its daily average. The important thing, however, is not to get faked out on the first or second day up and sucked into a premature rally, because you don't really know for sure whether the market has turned until you get that confirmation.

The tremendous added value of this system we created is not just that it will help you retreat from a topping general market and get in on the next bull market off the bottom. It can also keep you in cash during many of the false rallies that never follow through properly. This practical concept has several huge advantages. There have been two or three bear markets (or declines of 18 to 20 percent or more in one or more key averages) where the market, from the time it topped until it hit rock bottom, never experienced a valid follow-through day during its many attempted rallies until the actual bottom was made in the stock market.

A declining market will often rally for a few days, and the first day that volume picks up with the averages closing down can in many (but not all) cases be the start of the rally's failure and resumption of the downtrend.

What's important to understand is that no new bull market has ever started without a follow-through day, and most follow-throughs have come on the fourth through seventh days of rally attempts. With this knowledge, you have a system we designed and developed that can get you into the market four to seven days from the bottom. You're never going to do much better with any other technique, and you'll probably be much later if you go by the news (which will be terrible) or how you feel (which won't be much better).

Through the years, I've found that when you get a follow-through, the vast majority of investors simply do not believe it's for real. They are scared to death. They're too busy licking their wounds from a downtrend that's been so bad and news that's so negative that they're conditioned to doubt and be afraid of every rally. Here again, what's crucial is not how you feel at this fearful time or what you think, but that you recognize and understand what the market index itself is actually telling you. And if the market has followed through on a fourth, fifth, sixth, or seventh day, with an increase in volume, it's saying: "I'm now starting a whole new uptrend—regardless of what your hopes, fears, or personal opinions may be."

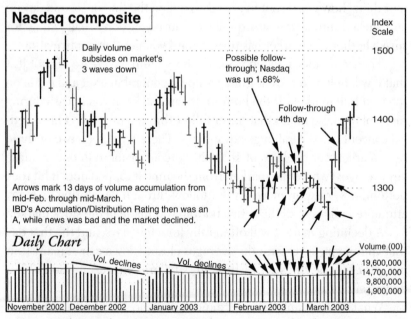

The March 2003 Bottom Amid Uncertainty and Bad News

You may have had one feeling about the market four or five weeks ago. But if the market has suddenly changed, you have to realize that. You can't keep the same thought you had before. If you do, you're arguing with the market, and that will usually cost you money. You must become flexible and able to shift and change your mind on a dime when the market changes. You can't afford to be consistent because the market is not consistent. What you said or stubbornly believed several weeks ago is totally irrelevant and never worth defending once the market changes direction. Have no pride of opinion or ego. As Emerson said, "A foolish consistency is the hobgoblin of little minds." The best generals on the battlefield react quickly and change plans based on what the enemy is doing, the weather, new or unexpected circumstances, or failures and mistakes that occur. The key for you is to be right when it's most important to be right on the market. And that's at all of the vital turning points in the major averages.

Some of the biggest profits in the markets are made by buying the first stocks that move to new high ground as you get a market follow-through. These are normally the new leaders in the new bull phase, and they'll go up farther and faster than other stocks even after the others eventually gather momentum. But these new leaders classically don't show up and identify themselves until the market has definitely hit bottom and turned. They continually evolve from proper patterns for up to the following three months. At that point, instead of dismissing the new rally, you're hard at work looking for and buying the new leaders. You're not waiting until the new uptrend eventually becomes obvious to everyone else. That will come months later, and at much higher prices.

My experience over many years is that follow-through days work 80 percent of the time. In the other 20 percent of cases, the follow-through will fizzle, usually within a few days, with the indexes closing down on increased volume.

Any system or set of rules that works 75 or 80 percent of the time is reliable enough to be used profitably. And it is certainly better than having no system or rules at all and just relying on how you feel or the opinions of others who probably have the same feelings.

In the 2000 to 2002 bear market, there were a few times when the follow-throughs fizzled several days later. But in nearly three years, two or three minor whipsaws (having to sell when you just started to get back in) were a very small price to pay for making sure you'd catch the next bull move at its earliest beginning point, when potentially new superwinners finally emerge.

The key thing to remember about this system is that you will never miss a major market top or a market bottom, and in most cases it will keep you out of numerous phony but costly premature rallies.

When we first tested and developed our system, we used models of every market top and bottom over the last 50 years. But the more severe the 2000 to 2002 decline got, the more we wondered how the system applied to the last time the market fell as much—namely, the 1929 to 1932 bear that ushered in the Great Depression. Sure enough, it picked the top on the second day after the peak in 1929. In other words: right smack on the button.

So much for another investment myth—that you can't time the market. By using this system, I was 100 percent out before the market topped in April 1962 and IBM proceeded to fall 50 percent. In the 1987 market, when it got so bad that the Dow plunged 500 points (over 22 percent at that time) in one day, we were 100 percent in cash long before things really started to fall apart. And in the 2000 to 2002 bear, we raised heavy amounts of cash in March 2000 based solely on our individual stock sell rules as well as distribution days in the mar-

Dow Jones Industrials 1974 Market Bottom Daily Chart

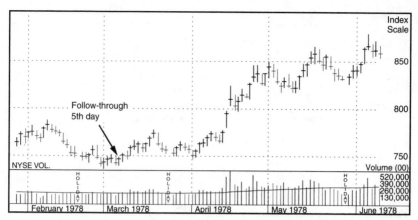

Dow Jones Industrials 1978 Market Bottom Daily Chart

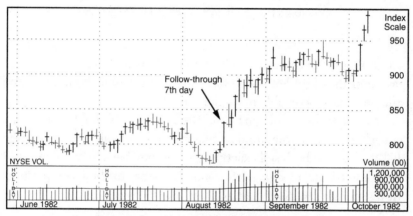

Dow Jones Industrials 1982 Market Bottom Daily Chart

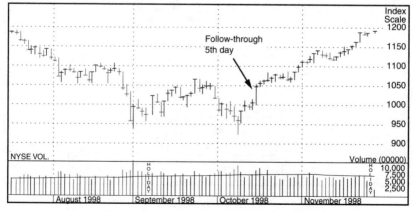

S&P 500 1998 Market Bottom Daily Chart

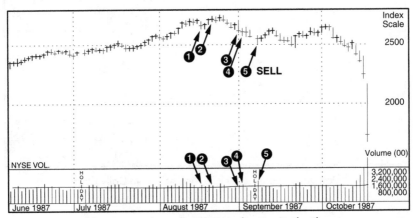

Dow Jones Industrials 1987 Market Top Daily Chart

ket averages. We've made this system work many times before in the past, and those students who have really done their homework and studied it have been able to do the same thing.

The myth that you can't time the market took hold many years ago, when a few mutual fund managers tried and failed. They learned that they had to both sell exactly right and buy back in exactly right if they didn't want to lose performance relative to their competitors. More specifically, they had to buy exactly right to get the same

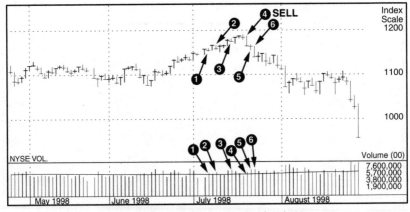

S&P 500 1998 Market Top Daily Chart

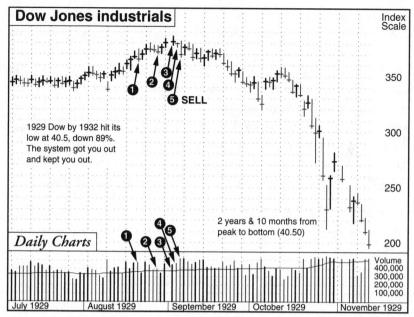

Dow Jones industrials

Index Scale

350

1929 Dow by 1932 hit its low at 40.5, down 89%. The system got you out and kept you out.

300

250

⑤ SELL

Daily Charts

2 years & 10 months from peak to bottom (40.50)

200

Volume
400,000
300,000
200,000
100,000

| July 1929 | August 1929 | September 1929 | October 1929 | November 1929 |

IBD's Market Distribution System Picks 1929 Top Two Days After Peak

bounceback effect of the rapid move off the bottom that their fully invested rivals normally enjoyed. This proved impossible because the funds were too big to quickly raise, say, 30 percent cash, or to get 30 percent cash back into the market.

It was then that managements of mutual fund companies started insisting that managers be fully (at least 95 percent) invested all the time. And out of that grew the fallacy that you can't time the market. The truth is that most mutual funds can't because they are too big, slow, and muscle-bound to gain the advantages offered by intelligent timing. You, as an agile individual investor who can retreat from or reenter the market without the size handicap, thus have a giant advantage.

The funds' policy of staying fully invested in the better stocks works pretty well for them in most bear markets, which correct only 20 to 25 percent. But there have been bears that correct 35 to 50 percent or more, and they can be devastating. Many individual stocks also suffer declines much larger than the percentage correction in the market indexes—all the more reason why you as an individual investor must have a time-proven system that helps you preserve and protect the hard-earned capital you worked many years to accumulate.

Even if it takes you a year or two to acquire real experience and skill with this simple system, think how much it could make or save you on your investment portfolio in the future once you've learned how to read what the market is actually doing. This knowledge and skill could protect and reward you and change your whole life. Anybody can learn to do it if they really want to and keep at it. And *IBD*'s "Big Picture" column is there to be your guide and instructor.

STEP 2

Use a Simple 3-to-1 Profit-and-Loss Percentage Plan

The main reason so many people lost so much money in the bear market of 2000 to 2002 is that they didn't know how to protect themselves from losses. They didn't know how to, or why they should, always and without exception cut and run when stocks they own fall below a certain percentage of their actual purchase price.

In other words, they didn't have a defense. They may have had a good offense, or thought they had a good offense, because they bought stocks they thought would go up. But they didn't have a set of rules that told them when to sell when their stocks were not acting right and started down.

In a moment, I'm going to give you a set of rules. If understood and followed correctly, these rules can forever keep you safe from all large, damaging losses even if just one of every three stocks you buy works out. And once that .333 batting average improves, the system can make you significant money.

Buying a stock without knowing when or why you should sell it is like buying a car with no brakes, or being in a boat with no life preservers, or taking flying lessons that teach you how to take off but not how to land. It's like having a baseball team with a lineup of great hitters who can't catch a cold when they take the field.

Most people who invest in the stock market think they're going to get rich without doing much homework or by listening to other people. They have no idea of the risks involved, let alone what they must do to lessen those risks. But they plow ahead anyway.

Sure, it would be nice if all we had to do is buy a "good" stock, sit back, and watch it magically go up and up and up. And I'll admit there were times in the crazy bubble market of the 1990s when that seemed to be the case. But, as so many people learned the hard way, it doesn't work like that at all.

What you must realize is that there are no "good" or "safe" stocks. In a way, all stocks are *bad*—that is, unless they go up. The only way your selections should be thought of as good stocks is after they prove themselves to be good by going up in price after you buy them. They must produce results.

Yes, there are stocks that go up a lot. They're the ones you should seek out. (We'll talk about how to find them in the following chapters.) But even great stocks don't stay great forever. Our studies of all the best stocks of the last 50 years show that the period of greatest market performance lasts on average only about a year and a half to two years. Some last up to three years. Only a tiny number last for 5 or 10 years. Even the best stocks eventually go down. And when they do, they can hurt you as much as, or even more than, the mediocre ones, especially if you buy them too late, as so many investors did as the 1990s bull market finally fizzled.

True market leaders—stocks that outperform all the rest by doubling or tripling or more—fall by an average 72 percent once they reach their peaks. And that's the *average* decline of all big leaders of each market cycle for the last 50 years. Many of the high-tech leaders in the 1990s markets lost more than 90 percent of their value.

But, you say, don't they all come back after a while? The answer, unfortunately for those who sit with them, is no. Nearly half of these market leaders never recover to their former peaks, and those that do take almost five years to do so. Some of the biggest winners can take much longer than that.

Investors who think the great leaders of the 1990s will snap back quickly should know that the leaders in a similar period of psycholog-

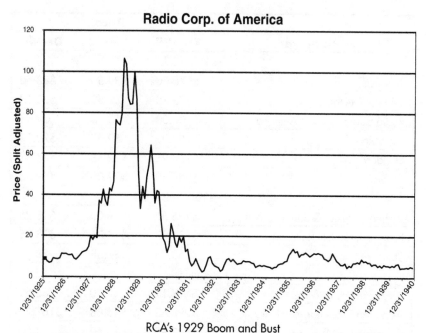

Radio Corp. of America

RCA's 1929 Boom and Bust

ical excess—the 1920s—didn't fully recover from the terrible 1929 to 1932 bear market until the 1940s or 1950s. For example, RCA, which soared over 1100 percent (from $8.70 to over $106) during the late 1920s, plunged to under $3 by 1932 and didn't see its pre-Crash level again until well after World War II (1963).

The RCA of the 1920s was very much like the AOLs and Ciscos of the 1990s: a leader in ushering in a new communications technology (in this case, radio, with its first commercial broadcast in 1920) that changed lives in much the same way the Internet did in the most recent decade. And, as the following table shows, RCA wasn't the only leader from the Roaring Twenties that fell hard and took a long time to get back on its feet.

Remember this key historical fact: only one of every eight leaders in a bull market reasserts itself as a leader in the next or a future bull phase. Times change, and along with them economic and competitive conditions. And the market normally moves on to new leadership.

Stock name	Price		
	Aug-29	**Jun-32**	**Dec-40**
Dow Jones industrials			
American Can	$178.00	$32.50	$88.50
General Electric	$98.88	$9.50	$33.13
Radio Corporation of America	$100.00	$3.25	$4.63
Sears Roebuck	$157.02	$9.97	$78.13
Standard Oil	$68.96	$22.58	$34.38
US Steel	$256.50	$22.00	$69.63
Dow Jones railroads			
Atchison Topeka & Santa Fe Rail	$295.50	$19.00	$18.25
New York Central Railroad	$231.97	$10.76	$13.75
Southern Pacific	$153.75	$7.38	$8.13
Dow Jones utilities			
American Power & Light	$117.19	$4.00	$2.50
American Telephone & Telegraph	$298.63	$76.88	$167.25
Columbia Gas Systems	$62.95	$5.50	$4.50
International Telephone & Telegraph	$142.01	$3.25	$1.88
Pacific Gas & Electric	$78.20	$18.75	$27.50

How 1929's Leaders Recovered by December 1940
(*Data Source:* © CRSP, Center for Research in Security Prices. The University of Chicago,
Graduate School of Business. Used with permission. All rights reserved.)

When you think about it and understand how our economic system works, the reasons for this are fairly simple. Our system is based on freedom and unlimited opportunity for anyone willing to work hard to achieve his or her dreams. You can win if you are determined and make up your mind to succeed. It doesn't matter who you are, what you look like, or where you come from, you can do it. Ambitious people from every country in the world come here to take advantage of this amazing opportunity, and their contributions add to our nation's diverse strength.

The most outstanding innovators, inventors, and entrepreneurs are relatively few in number—maybe 1 million in all. But when conditions are right—when tax and other government policies and regulations, for instance, encourage and help innovators rather than discourage them—they'll start new small companies that end up creating up to 80 to 90 percent or more of all new jobs as well as most new products, technologies, and future industries.

Later, a few of these fledging profitable companies will sell shares to the public in order to raise money to further finance their growth. And some of these new issues (called initial public offerings or IPOs) will establish themselves as market leaders. **In the bull market of the 1990s, four of every five market leaders were new companies that went public during the 1980s and early 1990s due in part to the lowering of the capital gains tax rate on corporate securities.** This fresh blood acts as a critical revitalizing force in each new market cycle as mutual funds and other institutional investors pile into the dynamic, faster-growing new leaders that are based on unique new products or inventions. This buying, in turn, eventually drives the stocks to the point where their price-to-earnings (PE) ratios—the most common measurement of a stock's current value—are more than twice what they were when the stocks started their remarkable price moves.

There comes a point, however, when these newer entrepreneurial companies either saturate their markets, attract more competitors (including some with even newer, better, or cheaper products or technologies), get carried away and overexpand, or simply grow so large that it becomes impossible to keep growing at the prior high rates. That's when the tide changes, and when some of the big mutual funds that piled into the stocks now start to pile out. After this process winds down, and our economy readjusts for previous excesses, a new cycle begins. It will be led in large part by a fresh group of innovative new companies with exciting new products or technological inventions. The pace of change and growth in America continues to accelerate. It is therefore vital for our future economy and market that this flow of newer companies (IPOs) continues. At this writing, IPOs are few.

It's also important that you understand the powerful role that mutual funds and other institutional investors play in determining market direction. When I read or hear typical news reports on a day's stock market activity, I'm always amused to hear how "investors" were worried about this or encouraged about that—as though individual investors had something to do with what happened. The fact is, the influence of individual investors on a stock's market direction is virtually nil.

So you just bought 200 shares of this, or your Aunt Sally sold 500 of that, or your pal Bob down at work unloaded 1000 of something else. Big deal! There are funds out there buying or selling 50,000 of this and 100,000 of that and 200,000 of something else, and their trades can dominate over yours, Sally's, Bob's, and those of every other individual.

Institutional, or professional, investors—many of whom manage portfolios in the tens of billions of dollars—account for about 75 percent of all important market activity (if you omit program trading). In most cases, it's their actions—and their actions only—that matter. Now, it would be nice to know how they feel, or what they're worried about, or what they see ahead, though they make plenty of mistakes too. But they're not about to tell you. Sure, you'll see some interviewed on TV. But most aren't. And it's my experience from working with hundreds of them over the last 40 years that the most successful ones—the real experts—are seldom seen or heard. They're too busy making important decisions based on research that the public has neither the time nor the resources to carry out. And the last thing they want to do is go on national TV and tell everybody what they're up to.

There's a reason they need to keep a low profile. It has to do with how big institutions are forced to go about their work. You and I can go into the market and get a 200-, 500-, or 1000-share order filled in minutes. But it's much different for a fund that has tens of millions, or hundreds of millions, or especially billions of dollars under management.

Say the fund runs $5 billion in assets, and it wants to own a 2 percent position in the fund in a certain stock. That means it needs to buy $100 million worth of the shares. Let's also say it's a $50 stock. So that's 2 million shares the fund will have to buy. Now let's say the stock's average daily trading volume is 1 million shares. And let's say the fund is going to buy 5 percent, or 50,000, of the shares that change hands each day. This means that, with 22 trading days a month, it'll take the fund two months of buying to acquire its 2 percent position. And that's if it's in there buying every day, which it probably isn't. More likely, it'll buy for several days, then back off for a day or two, letting the price come down a little, and then resume its buying. This process may stretch the period needed to accumulate the position out to three months.

The steady accumulation of the stock by this fund, and others like it, is what pushes the price up. That's why it's important for you to recognize professional buying when you see it—a subject we'll cover in the next chapter. But for the purposes of this chapter, it's just as important to recognize professional selling when you see it, because it's the selling, or distribution, of stock in the quantities that institutions deal with that drives share prices down.

As reluctant as institutions are to talk about what they're buying, they're even more reluctant to discuss what they're getting rid of. The reason is obvious: if others know that the professionals who really determine a stock's direction are bailing out, they too will sell. The price will come down that much faster, and the institutions, which can't get out quickly, will be forced to accept lower and lower prices for the many thousands of shares they must distribute when they can. This really gives the fast-thinking individual investor a huge advantage— provided, of course, that he or she can recognize when institutions are heading for the exit.

At this juncture, it's especially important that you learn to ignore your own feelings and the opinions of others. When you see your stock moving against you, you must be totally objective. You may hear someone on TV opine that the company whose stock you own is still great, and that the fact that it's now at $50 instead of $80 makes it a bargain. After watching your stock fall 37.5 percent, this expert's opinion may help soothe your jangled nerves. But the market doesn't care about how you feel or what that supposed expert thinks. The only opinion you should be interested in is that of the market itself. Through its price and volume action, the market will be clearly telling you what the professionals are doing.

In this case, the fact that your stock has fallen from $80 to $50 means something is wrong. Some institutions are selling. You may not know why; in fact, it's likely you won't know. But you can't afford to wait for the specifics. By the time the news is out, you may be down so much you'll never recover.

That's what happened to millions of investors when the bubble burst in 2000. Many of the phenomenal leaders of the 1990s market—

the stocks that everybody had to own, and eventually did own—were topping in February and March. But few seemed to notice. Instead, "experts" were still advising people to buy. Even worse, they were advising them to buy more—to "buy on the dips"—as the stocks got "cheaper." You'd better write that one down: the phrase *buy on dips* can be an invitation to disaster, just as the shallow phrase *it's a good buy* could mean "good-bye money."

Making all of this easier was the fact that the earnings of many of these market-leading companies were up 100 percent in the preceding quarter and Wall Street analysts were projecting more of the same in the quarter to follow.

By the time results finally came out showing earnings down for the first time, the stocks were off 50 to 60 percent. Then the selling really kicked in, driving the prices down to levels shareholders never thought they'd see in their worst nightmares.

If you let a stock you own drop 50 or 60 percent—or even 25 or 30 percent—from your purchase price, you need to realize how big a hole you've dug for yourself. Let's use that $80 stock that's now $50 as

Earnings per Share Look Great at the Top, up 350 Percent

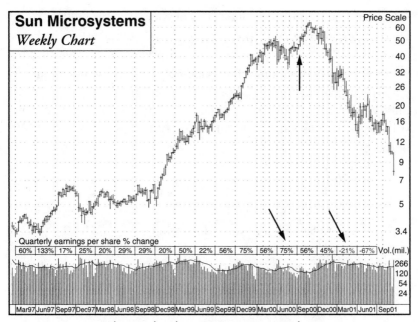

Sun Microsystems
Weekly Chart

Price Scale
60
50
40
32
26
20
16
12
9
7
5
3.4

Quarterly earnings per share % change

60%	133%	17%	25%	20%	29%	29%	20%	50%	22%	56%	75%	56%	75%	56%	45%	-21%	-67%

Vol.(mil.)
266
120
54
24

| Mar97 | Jun97 | Sep97 | Dec97 | Mar98 | Jun98 | Sep98 | Dec98 | Mar99 | Jun99 | Sep99 | Dec99 | Mar00 | Jun00 | Sep00 | Dec00 | Mar01 | Jun01 | Sep01 |

Another Leader Shows Great Earnings at the Top

an example. To recoup your 37.5 percent loss, that stock—or, if you sell it, the next one you buy—will have to rally 60 percent (from $50 to $80). If you don't sell it (because it's now such a "bargain"), and it falls to $40 (an even bigger "bargain"), you'll need it to double to get back even. And if you let it drop 75 percent, you need 300 percent to get back in the game! Do you realize how few stocks go up 300 percent or even 100 percent?

Remember: leading stocks (the kind you should be looking for) correct an average 72 percent after they've topped. And many of the big leaders of the 1990s corrected much more than that. The chances of a stock quadrupling (+300 percent) to get you back to even are remote at best. And the odds aren't much better that the next stock you buy, even if it goes up, will achieve that kind of gain.

So what can you do to protect yourself against catastrophic losses that can and do happen to almost all investors? I know of only one sure way, and that's to have a realistic plan of selling and taking profits on the way up, while a stock is still advancing, and selling and cutting every loss very short when a stock starts off poorly and goes against you. Specifi-

25

cally, you should consider selling a few of your stocks when they are up 20 to 25 percent from your purchase price and cutting every single loss at no more than 7 or 8 percent. The sell price profit target, in other words, is roughly three times the mandatory loss recognition point.

By maintaining this 3-to-1 profit-vs.-loss ratio, you can be right on only 30 percent of your stock purchases and wrong on 70 percent and still not get into serious trouble. Here's a simple example using $5000 of capital:

> *Trade 1*
> You buy 100 shares of a $50 stock . . . $5000
> . . . but it goes down 7 percent . . .   −$350
> . . . to $46.50, and you sell, leaving: $4650
>
> *Trade 2*
> You buy 100 shares of a $46.50 stock . . . $4650
> . . . but it too goes down 7 percent . . .   −$326
> . . . to $43.24, and you sell, leaving: $4324
>
> *Trade 3*
> You buy 100 shares of a $43.24 stock . . . $4324
> . . . and this one goes up 20 percent . . .   +$883
> . . . to $51.89, and you sell, leaving: $5189

The commissions from these six (three round-trip) trades will probably run from $60 for a deep discount broker to $600 or more for a full-service broker. Taking an average of $50 a trade, for total transaction costs of $300, you are left with the same $5000 you started with.

Once you learn to buy stocks properly (which we'll discuss in the next chapter), you should be right on one-half to two-thirds of your trades. But until you reach that point, this discipline—cutting losses at 7 or 8 percent and taking profits at 20 to 25 percent—will keep you in the game even if you're right on only one of three transactions.

Once you're batting .500, moreover, this discipline will help get you ahead. For example:

> *Trade 1*
> You buy 100 shares of a $50 stock . . . $5000
> . . . but it goes down 7 percent . . .   −$350
> . . . to $46.50, and you sell, leaving: $4650

Trade 2

You buy 100 shares of a $46.50 stock . . .	$4650
. . . and it goes up 20 percent . . .	+$950
. . . to $55.80, and you sell, leaving:	$5580

Trade 3

You buy 100 shares of a $55.80 stock . . .	$5580
. . . and it goes down 7 percent . . .	−$391
. . . to $51.91, and you sell and take the profit, leaving:	$5191

Trade 4

You buy 100 shares of a $51.91 stock . . .	$5191
. . . and it goes up 20 percent . . .	+$1038
. . . to $62.29, and you sell, leaving:	$6229

Deducting $400 for commissions (eight $50 transactions), you have $5960, or 19 percent more than you started with.

String together a few gains of 20 or 25 percent and it gets better yet. Three gains of 25 percent, for example, compound to a 90 percent profit. And on 50 percent margin (using money borrowed from your brokerage firm) in a strong bull market, your gain swells to 180 percent.

We'll talk later about a key rule that will let your profits run in the stocks you buy that advance 20 percent in only one, two, or three weeks immediately after their purchase. It's those stocks that often turn out to be the home run hitters in your lineup. Meantime, the simple 3-to-1 formula for offsetting losses with gains will provide all the defense you need. You'll also be gaining more irreplaceable market experience than if you just bought one stock and held it for a long time no matter how it performed.

In extremely difficult markets, when profits are harder to come by, you might want to pull in your parameters and reduce the size and exposure of your commitment. For example, you might sell when your stock is down only 3 to 5 percent, take profits at 10 to 15 percent, or commit a smaller proportion of your investible funds. But whatever you do, the key is maintaining the 3-to-1 ratio.

Be aware that when you sell at 7 or 8 percent below your cost, the stock may often turn around and rally to higher levels. When this happens, you'll feel like a fool. "This," you'll say to yourself, "just proves I was right about the stock in the first place, and that selling it was a mistake."

But was it really a mistake? What you're really doing when you sell at 7 or 8 percent is making absolutely sure you will never, ever suffer a catastrophic loss from which you can't recover. You are preventing that 7 or 8 percent from slipping to 15 or 20 percent, or 30 or 40 percent, or much worse. Think of it as just another form of insurance. You have fire insurance on your house, don't you? If your house didn't burn down last year, are you kicking yourself for having bought that insurance? Of course not. It's the same with cutting your losses short in the market. A 7 percent loss in a stock that sometimes turns around and runs up 20 percent is a small price to pay for ensuring that a 7 percent loss doesn't become a 70 percent loss that, like an uninsured house burnt to the ground, will take you years to recover from—if you ever recover.

All this buying and selling is fine, you might say, for those who speculate in stocks that carry greater risk. But what about the buy-and-hold long-term investor who deals in less volatile "blue-chip" or "investment-grade" issues? Well, I've got news for you: there's no such thing. All common stocks are highly speculative and can carry significant risk, including those widely viewed as safe. Many buy-and-hold long-term investors lost 50 to 75 percent from 2000 to 2003 because they had no sell rules.

When I started in the business over 40 years ago, most widows thought and were told that all you had to own was American Telephone & Telegraph. After all, it was a phone company, so it would never go out of business. And it was quality. And you got dividend income and stability. And your father had it, and your grandfather before him. Well, in January 1999, AT&T was $98.80 a share. But by July 2002, it was changing hands at $17—down 83 percent. So much for safety.

Texas Utilities, now known as TXU Corp, is another example. It fell from a peak of over $57 down to $10—a drop of 82 percent. And how about the California blue-chip utilities forced into bankruptcy due to the state's unbelievably poor micromanagement of the industry?

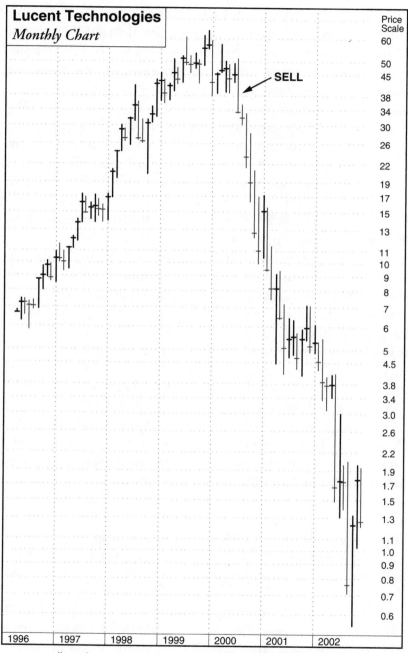

Lucent Technologies
Monthly Chart

Price Scale

SELL

1996 1997 1998 1999 2000 2001 2002

All Stocks Have Risk, That's Why You Must Cut Short All Losses

Then there was AT&T spin-off Lucent Technologies, one of the most widely held stocks in America. It was not only the largest supplier of telecommunications equipment in the world; it was home to the storied Bell Laboratories, producer of some of the most mind-boggling technological breakthroughs of our time. Lucent did well from the time it was spun off in 1996 until it topped at $64 in December 1999. But from there, it nosedived 98 percent, to less than $1 a share.

Lucent is no different from high fliers in earlier cycles, many of which disintegrated into $1 stocks if they didn't vanish altogether via merger or bankruptcy. In the 1960s, when color TV was introduced, Admiral quadrupled in 39 weeks. Today, you'd be hard pressed to find a U.S. company that still makes TVs. In the 1970s, Service Merchandise ran up 586 percent in 139 weeks. But when was the last time you shopped in a catalog showroom? In the late 1980s and 1990s, L. M. Ericsson soared with the use of cellular phones. But the Swedish company lost it all and then some in the 2000 to 2002 bear.

I remember when Xerox traded at $260 a share. In the fall of 2002, it was below $5. American Machine & Foundry, a big leader that sold at over $100 in the 1960s, was eventually delisted from the New York Stock Exchange. And those aren't the only household names to be treated so rudely. Here's a list of other blue chips and former leaders and how they did in the 2000 to 2002 market.

As you can see, there's risk in all common stocks, and today's blue chip can quickly become tomorrow's cow chip. Yes, through hindsight we can point to stocks like General Electric or Minnesota Mining & Manufacturing (3M), which have risen steadily over many years, and conclude, "Wow! All I have to do is find one of those and my troubles will be over." But true long-term growth stocks like GE and 3M are the rare exception, and the odds are you might end up instead with an Enron or WorldCom. Or, if you finally decide to buy GE, it could decline and underperform for the next five years. Leaders continually change.

Even if you are lucky enough to own a long-term winner, you'll probably have only one or two in what might be a portfolio of 10 or more stocks. Without strict sell rules and the discipline to execute them, how do you prevent losses in the others from eroding or even canceling out your gains in the few big producers?

Former stock leaders or blue chips	Time to bottom	Maximum percent off peak
AOL Time Warner	2½ years	91%
AT&T	3½ years	83%
Amazon.com	1¾ years	95%
Apple Computer	9 months	86%
Brunswick	2½ years	87%
Circuit City Stores	3 years	91%
Cisco Systems	2½ years	90%
Corning	2 years	99%
EMC	2 years	96%
Eastman Kodak	4¾ years	74%
Ericsson	2½ years	99%
FAO Schwarz	3 years	99%
Ford Motor	3½ years	83%
Gap	2¾ years	84%
General Electric	2 years	65%
Goodyear Tire & Rubber	5 years	96%
Home Depot	2¾ years	71%
Intel	2 years	83%
JC Penney	2¼ years	89%
JDS Uniphase	2½ years	99%
JP Morgan Chase	2½ years	77%
Kmart	10 years	99%
Mattel	2 years	81%
McDonald's	3¼ years	75%
Micron Technology	2½ years	93%
Nextel Communications	2¼ years	97%
Oracle	1¾ years	84%
Polaroid	2¼ years	91%
Qualcomm	2½ years	88%
Rite Aid	2 years	97%
Sprint Fon Group	2¾ years	91%
Sun Microsystems	2 years	96%
TXU	7 months	82%

Being a Long-Term Buy-and-Hold Investor Is Not Really the Safest Method!

Former stock leaders or blue chips	Time to bottom	Maximum percent off peak
Tellabs	2¾ years	95%
Texas Instruments	2½ years	87%
Tommy Hilfiger	3¾ years	86%
Tyco International	1½ years	89%
UAL	5 years	99%
Walt Disney	2¼ years	69%
Worldcom	3 years	99%
Xerox	1½ years	94%
Yahoo!	1¾ years	97%

Being a Long-Term Buy-and-Hold Investor Is Not Really the Safest Method! (*Continued*)

Most will say diversification is the answer—that spreading your money among many stocks makes it less likely that a few can do much damage. There's definitely some truth to that. But as both long-term and highly diversified investors can attest, there's also truth in the old adage, "When they raid the house, they get them all." In other words, bear markets like that of 2000 to 2002 will eventually take down all the leaders.

After the market topped early in 2000, Cisco Systems, one of the greatest stocks of our time or any other, held up and held up and held up—until September, when it too began to fall. Its legion of fans still can't believe that Cisco, which sold for $82 in March 2000, traded at $13 a year later (even as both profits and sales continued to grow at better than 55 percent a quarter) and eventually got as low as $8.

In short, it doesn't do much good to diversify into 20 or 30 stocks if all you're left with after a sharp bear market is 20 or 30 stocks down 50 percent overall. Some of the best mutual fund managers in 2000 to 2002 found their portfolios declined 50 to 60 percent or even more. Being widely diversified among 100 or more stocks did not protect them from substantial losses. So diversification is not realistically a foolproof guarantee of real safety.

The legendary investor Gerald Loeb wrote his first book in 1935, right in the middle of the Depression. So he knew widespread devastation first-hand. He concluded that broad diversification was a "hedge for ignorance." A sounder approach, in my opinion, is to own a smaller group of stocks, know them inside and out, and watch them so closely that, if something goes wrong, you waste no time in acting to correct the situation.

To repeat: all stocks should be considered bad unless they go up. And if they go down, it's up to you alone, if you're a self-directed investor (or you and your broker, if you use one) to act quickly enough before much damage is done. The problem is, neither of you will be so inclined.

Let's take you, for instance. Because you have so much invested in your stock—not only your money, but your pride, your ego, and your emotions—you won't want to let it go. And you'll come up with every excuse in the world before you do. "There's nothing wrong with my stock," you'll say, "it's the overall market that's having trouble." Or, "My company is doing fine, but the economy has run into a rough patch—and this, too, will pass." Or, "It's come down this far before and bounced back. No reason to think it won't come back again." Or, "They just reported great earnings. Everything's still on track." Eventually, you'll get to, "I'm a long-term investor, and the market always comes back," "It's come down this far, no way it can go lower," and, "Oh, well, I'm still getting my (2 percent) dividend," even though the stock itself is down 60 percent.

Rationalization of this kind is all too understandable. It's human nature. But to be successful in the market, you've absolutely got to get over it. You've got to suppress your emotions and let cold, hard objectivity and rules govern your decision making, because, again, the stock market doesn't care who you are or what you feel or fear or hope for.

"You hope when you should fear," said another great investor, Jesse Livermore, "and fear when you should hope." In other words, when your stock is up some, you should hope it'll go higher instead of fearing it'll stop going up and selling before it has a chance to complete its move. And when your stock is going down and losing money, you should fear it'll fall even more, instead of hoping beyond hope that it'll turn around and bail you out.

Making it even tougher to sell will be the many opinions you'll hear not only about your stock, but about the market or the economy in general. You'll hear "experts"—maybe the same experts you listened to when you bought the stock in the first place—insist it's still a great company, and that now that it's fallen several points, it's an even better buy than it was before. But again, these are just their personal opinions. And in the stock market, personal opinions aren't worth diddly-squat. The only opinion you need to heed is that of the market itself. It's going to go wherever it wants, because it's based purely on supply and demand, and it's up to you to make sure it doesn't take you to a place you can't get back from.

As for your broker, he or she also must have the courage to recommend decisive action. But if he doesn't, you've got to understand where he's coming from. He might have put 50 customers in the same stock he put you in. And you can imagine what he's going to go through as he calls every customer and admits that a mistake has been made and will have to be corrected as soon as possible. It's an unenviable task at best. He'll have to deal with all the psychological hang-ups that the self-directed individual investor has to overcome. Most can't do this. This is why you and your broker should have an understanding from the start that there will be times—and they will occur quite often— when you'll have to sell something you both agreed to buy, and that it's all part of investing.

This is definitely the toughest lesson all investors have to learn, and many never learn it, which is why so many never produce more than mediocre results. However, if you use the more realistic system I've just shown you, your risk in any stock will never be more than 7 to 8 percent.

How to Buy the Very Best Stocks at the Very Best Time

Now that you know how to protect yourself with a simple profit-and-loss plan, let me give you a dozen rules that will help you pick the very best stocks when they have the best chance of being real winners and when you have the least chance of making a bad mistake in the course of a bull (clear uptrending) market.

These rules aren't based on my personal opinions or feelings or those of Wall Street analysts. They're based on characteristics shared by nearly all the biggest winners of each year over the last half century—the stocks that advanced 100 to 1000 percent or more.

And by *more,* I mean as much as 75,000 percent, which was the gain for Cisco Systems from the time it came public in 1990 until it topped in early 2000. This gain was big enough to turn a $3,000 investment in 100 shares into over $202 million. Other examples are the 485 percent increase achieved by AOL in only six months from October 1998 to April 1999, or the 2500 percent profit made by Qualcomm from late 1998 to the end of 1999.

In other words, these rules are based on how the stock market actually works in reality, rather than on how the majority of people think it works.

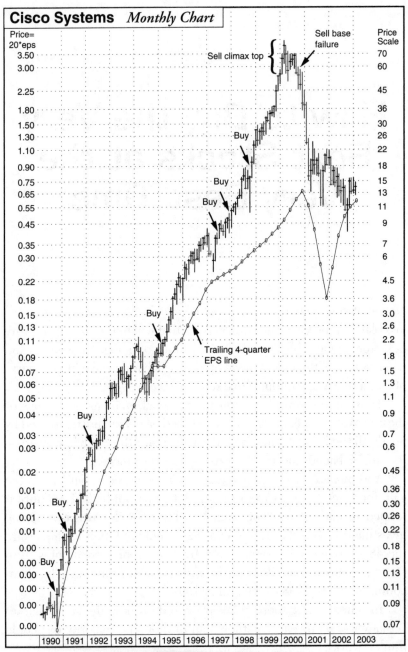

Cisco Systems *Monthly Chart*

Price=
20*eps

Sell climax top

Sell base failure

Price Scale

Buy

Buy

Buy

Buy

Trailing 4-quarter
EPS line

Buy

Buy

Buy

1990 1991 1992 1993 1994 1995 1996 1997 1998 1999 2000 2001 2002 2003

Cisco Systems up 75,000 Percent from 1990 to 2000

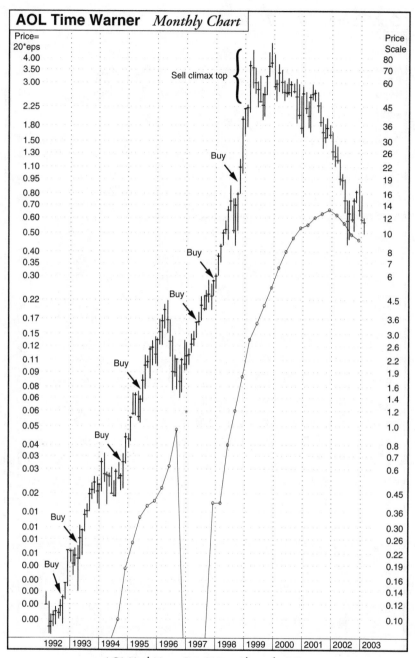

AOL Had Many Buy Points Along the Way

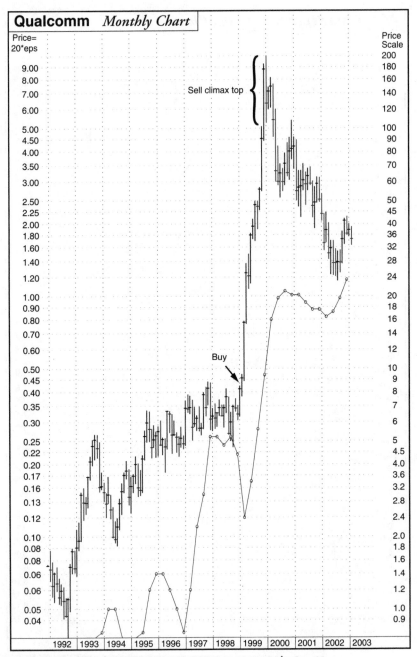

Qualcomm Was up 2,567 Percent in Only One Year

1. Earnings per share in the latest quarter should be up at least 25 percent versus the same quarter a year ago, and preferably much more.

Of all the factors that affect stock price, profitability is the most important. And earnings per share (EPS) is the way profitability is measured. They're calculated by dividing a company's total after-tax profits by the number of shares outstanding.

2. Earnings growth should be accelerating at some point in recent quarters compared with earlier rates of change.

By *accelerating*, I mean percentage gains in earnings per share that exceed those of prior quarters—for example, a company that's been growing at 25 percent for several quarters and suddenly starts growing at 40 percent. In some cases that growth could have lasted two or three quarters or more.

The acceleration doesn't always have to occur in the latest period. It could have started up to six or eight quarters ago. But somewhere, currently or in the recent past, you should see a definite pickup in the percentage rate of earnings improvement. What you're looking for is a company that's been growing steadily but suddenly is doing significantly better. The market is always interested in what's looking better and improving.

3. Annual earnings for the last three years should be increasing at a rate of 25 percent per year or even more.

If the stock is a younger company that recently had its IPO and doesn't have three years of positive earnings growth, you might accept the last five or six quarters of earnings and sales being up a significant amount.

Another time-saving way to evaluate a company's three-year earnings growth and its percentage increase in earnings in recent quarters is to use *Investor's Business Daily's* EPS Rating, which measures precisely those two factors. (Stocks that rate 95 or higher in all of IBD's stock tables are normally better prospects.)

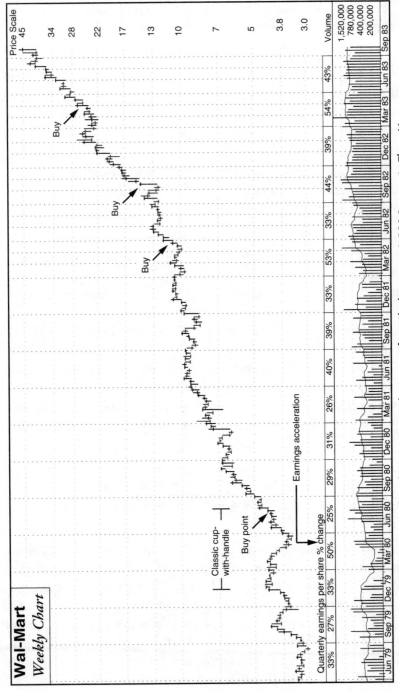

Wal-Mart Displayed Earnings Acceleration Before Climbing over 1,000 Percent in Three Years

4. Sales should be up 25 percent or more in one or more recent quarters, or at least accelerating in their percentage change for the last three quarters.

The progression could be from a –5 percent to a +10 percent to a +30 percent. For a company's growth to be sustainable, it's important to have both strong or accelerating sales and improving earnings. One without the other is not reliable.

5. The after-tax profit margin in the most recent quarter should be either at or at least close to a new high and among the very best in the company's industry.

Retailing is an industry that tends to have low margins. But here, too, you want retailers with the best margins in the group. During their periods of great success, Wal-Mart and Home Depot showed pretax margins of 6 percent and 3.8 percent, respectively. Outside retailing, the best historical stock performers have had annual pretax margins of 18 percent or higher.

6. Return on equity should be 15 to 17 percent or higher.

Return on equity (ROE) measures how efficient a company is with its money. Most outstanding growth leaders in past market cycles have shown a return on equity of 15 to 17 percent or higher.

In all these examples, you can assume the higher the better. A 25 percent ROE is better than 17 percent, and 35 or 40 percent is better than 25 percent.

7. Technology companies should show cash flow earnings per share greater than regular earnings.

Cash flow adds back the amount of depreciation a company shows to reflect the amount of cash being generated internally. Growth companies in general, and tech companies in particular, will show cash flow 20 percent or greater than the actual annual earnings per share.

Stock name	Return on equity at the time	Year an up move started	Percent increase to peak
Pic 'N Save	28.7%	1976	2950%
Home Depot	27.8%	1982	958%
PriceCo	55.4%	1982	1086%
Liz Claiborne	42.4%	1984	715%
The Limited	42.3%	1985	451%
This Can't Be Yogurt	41.2%	1985	2073%
Merck	19.8%	1985	870%
Microsoft	40.5%	1986	340%
Cisco	36.3%	1990	74,445%
International Game Technology	22.9%	1991	1691%
Nokia	30.9%	1998	862%
QLogic	18.8%	1998	3345%
America Online	36.3%	1998	481%
Charles Schwab	29.4%	1998	434%

The Importance of a Strong Return on Equity

Where do you find this information that you can trust? At investors.com we have charts available on stocks, and the Daily Graphs® investment research tool has a lot of additional information, such as ROE, which is a pretty basic measurement used by most accountants. It may not be available in some reports, but it's surely available if you do some checking. ROE is important because it's another measure of profitability and growth in a company.

8. In normal bull markets, both the earnings per share and relative strength ratings should in most cases be 90 or higher.

The EPS Rating is calculated by combining a company's three-year rate of profit growth with recent quarterly earnings to provide one simple measure to assess short- and long-term profitability growth. *Investor's Business Daily's* EPS Ratings run from 1 to 99, with 99 being the best.

If a company has an EPS Rating of 95, that means its earnings growth over the last three years, with added weight given to recent quarters, has been superior to that of 95 percent of all publicly held companies. In some cases, you might accept an EPS Rating as low as 80. However, as with the other measures we've discussed, the higher the better. Companies with EPS Ratings of 95 to 99 are generally better during bull markets than those with 85s. In November 1990, before Cisco began its 75,000 percent advance, its EPS Rating in *Investor's Business Daily's* stock tables was 99 and its relative price strength was 97.

The Relative Strength Rating measures stock price performance over the past 12 months. A rating of 90 means that a company's stock has outperformed 90 percent of all others over that period. The stocks you buy should have a strong EPS Rating plus a strong Relative Strength Rating, *not just one or the other.* In the early beginning phase of a new bull market after an abnormally steep bear market, as in 2000 to 2002, a six-month relative strength measure might be of some value or at least provide a second view of relative price action.

IBD's "Friday Weekly Review" section includes charts and a screen that lists companies rated 85 or higher in Earnings Per Share and Relative Strength Rating. The stocks on this list have tended to outperform most of the well-known stock indexes over many years.

Every Monday in the B section, IBD features the top 100 companies in terms of EPS and Relative Strength Ratings together with a description of each company or an update on recent company news. This could serve as a prospect list of companies worthy of following via charts and further fundamental study.

9. The stock's industry group should rank in the top 10 or 20 among the 197 groups tracked by *Investor's Business Daily.*

You want most of your stocks to be part of groups that are in the top 20 of the 197 industries tracked by *Investor's Business Daily.* As already noted, only 5 or 10 industries will lead every bull market, but some related industries may also do well. If there's a building boom under way, for example, and all the home building stocks are going up, so might mortgage financiers or makers of lawn mowers or wash-

197 Industry Groups*	
(Dec. 31, 1998)	
Group rank	**Industry group**
1	Computer Software—Internet
2	Electronic Semiconductor Manufacturing
3	Computer—Memory Devices
4	Retail/Wholesale—Computers/Cell
5	Computer—Local Networks
6	Electronic—Misc. Components
7	Electronic—Semiconductor Equipment
8	Computer—Mini/Micro
9	Retail—Mail Order and Direct
10	Computer—Mainframes
11	Computer Software—Enterprise
12	Computer Software—Desktop
13	Food—Meat Products
14	Media—Cable TV
15	Medical—Biomedical/Genetics
16	Retail—Consumer Electronics
17	Medical—Products
18	Media—Books
19	Computer Software—Security
20	Medical—Wholesale Drug/Sundry

197 Industry Groups	
(March 28, 2003)	
Group rank	**Industry group**
1	Telecommunications—Fiber Optics
2	Internet—ISP
3	Electronic Semiconductor Manufacturing
4	Internet—E-Commerce
5	Telecommunications—Wireless Equipment
6	Media—Cable/Satellite TV
7	Internet—Content
8	Computer—Data Storage
9	Computer—Software Enterprise
10	Computer—Desktop
11	Medical—Generic Drugs
12	Computer—Software Medical
13	Transportation—Services
14	Computer—Networking
15	Banks—Southeast
16	Machinery—Material Handling/Automation
17	Medical—Products
18	Banks—Northeast
19	Telecommunications—Wireless Services
20	Banks—Foreign

*The William O'Neil + Co. 197 Industry Groups™ is a trademark owned by William O'Neil + Co., Inc., and is used by IBD under license agreement.

197 Industry Groups Are Ranked 1 (Best) Through 197 (Worst)

ing machines. What you're looking for is the strongest segment of each leading sector. If your stock is not in a top-performing group, at least one or two other stocks in its industry group should have high EPS and relative strength ratings. Sixty percent of the best winning stocks historically have been part of a strong industry group move.

10. The stock should have institutional sponsors—such as mutual funds, banks, and insurance companies—and the number of mutual fund sponsors should be increasing quarter by quarter for several quarters.

You should also see that at least a few of the best-performing mutual funds have bought the stock as a new holding or as a significant addition to an existing position in the last quarter or two.

11. It's usually a plus if the company is buying back its own stock—preferably 5 to 10 percent or more.

If a stock has all the other positive CAN SLIM characteristics, and if the company is buying back shares, there's a strong probability management expects improved earnings in the future. In cases where a buyback is not happening, insist that management own a reasonable number of shares. It's hard to generalize about the percentage management should own. In big, well-established companies with many shares outstanding, 2 percent may be enough. In younger companies with a more limited number of shares, management ownership might range from 5 to 30 percent or so.

12. It's vital in any stock you buy that you really understand the story of the company.

What does the company make or do? How are its products or services used? What unique advantages do they offer? Who buys them? In short, really understand what you own. The better you know the company, and the more you believe in it, the more likely you are to make sound decisions, and the more able you'll be to stay with the stock through normal corrections. This is not to say that you should blindly hang on if the stock is not working out as expected. Always pay attention to what the market is telling you about your stocks.

An overarching concept here is that as much as possible you should pick the company that is number 1 in its industry or particular field. Notice I didn't say number 1 in name recognition or brand awareness, but number 1 in terms of current key measurements such as EPS growth, return on equity, profit margins, sales growth, and relative price performance of the company's stock. Everyone knows and recognizes Sears, but are its fundamental performance numbers saying it's number 1 in the retail industry today? Look for the real present-day leaders. New ones continually emerge.

Once you've isolated the very best companies via a custom screening and have done a detailed comparison of each company's key variables, you need to determine when is the absolute best time to buy their stock. At what point, in other words, does the stock stand the best chance of increasing in price soon and becoming a potential big winner? This doesn't mean when the stock is cheapest; it means when its percentage chance of significant success is greatest.

By far the easiest and most efficient way to make this determination is by using charts along with your fundamental data. Charts let you monitor hundreds of securities that otherwise would be impossible for you to keep track of. The charts we'll show you as examples are all adjusted for stock splits, so don't think we're suggesting you should buy lower-priced stocks. Most that show a $5 or $10 beginning price were likely $30 to $50 at that point in time.

I mainly use daily and weekly price and volume charts. But I'll also refer to monthly charts and even intraday charts covering intervals as brief as 5 or 10 minutes. I prefer weeklies because they provide a good overall practical perspective and it's easier to spot sound patterns. I'll always check a daily chart, too, so I don't miss key price or volume buying clues that occur on one or two days at important points that might not show up on the weekly. It also helps to check out the monthly charts covering a period of many years. A stock could be emerging out of a 10-year base and old price high as well as a shorter-term proper pattern, which could add to its potential.

Many new investment ideas can be picked up by scanning a large number of charts that are first screened against the extensive IBD database, or some other database, for the best fundamental characteristics. Look for the following five basic chart patterns.

Cup with a handle.   That's what we nicknamed the pattern, or base, we found most often in the best stocks of the last 50 years. It looks like the silhouette of a cup when viewed from the side.

The typical cup-with-a-handle pattern corrects with the stock moving down five to seven weeks to form the left side of the cup. Sometimes it's longer, sometimes shorter. Most cups round out around the bottom for a few weeks, but some bottom areas are more narrow. Then they move up on the right side, getting more than halfway up the pattern, usually to within 10 or 15 percent of the pattern's old high price. Then the plot starts moving sideways, drifting off in what we call the handle area of the pattern. Trading volume in the lower part of the handle and for a week or two along the bottom of the cup frequently declines or dries up to a very low level. This means there's not much more selling coming into the stock at that point, which is a constructive factor.

The best time to buy these stocks during a bull market is after the handle, which should have been drifting down along its price lows, has been completed and the stock starts to move back up, getting ready to break out of the earlier recorded peak price in the handle area. This is called the pivot or precise buy point. It may be referred to as a new high. However, it is typically 5, 10, or 15 percent away from the absolute peak price in the overall cup-with-handle pattern. The strongest cup-with-a-handle patterns will always show a powerful prior uptrend in price of at least 30 percent on large, increased volume over many weeks in the uptrend.

Following are three classic examples of cup-with-a-handle patterns formed during the 1998 to 2000 bull market, with the buy points and subsequent advances noted. I have also placed faulty cup-with-a-handle patterns afterward that appear to be similar but actually possess defects that caused them to fail and decline in price.

Cup-with-a-handle patterns weren't peculiar to the 1998 to 2000 period. They have appeared and reappeared continuously in every cycle throughout market history.

A cup-with-a-handle base should be at least six to eight weeks in length, starting with the first week closing down off the stock's top.

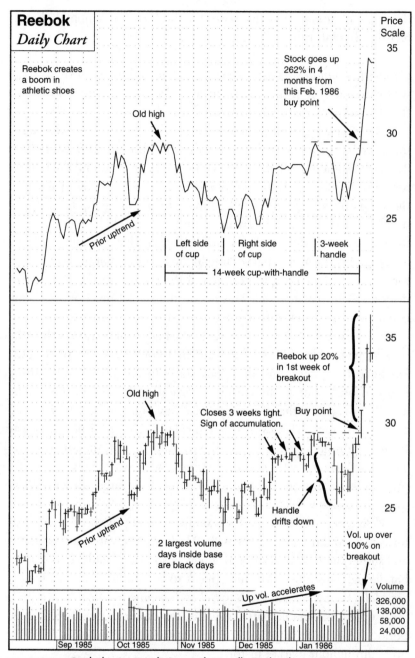

Reebok
Daily Chart

Price Scale

Reebok creates a boom in athletic shoes

Stock goes up 262% in 4 months from this Feb. 1986 buy point

35

Old high

30

Prior uptrend

25

Left side of cup | Right side of cup | 3-week handle

14-week cup-with-handle

35

Reebok up 20% in 1st week of breakout

Old high

Closes 3 weeks tight. Sign of accumulation.

Buy point

30

Prior uptrend

Handle drifts down

25

2 largest volume days inside base are black days

Vol. up over 100% on breakout

Up vol. accelerates

Volume

326,000
138,000
58,000
24,000

Sep 1985 | Oct 1985 | Nov 1985 | Dec 1985 | Jan 1986

Reebok's 14-Week Cup-with-Handle Daily Chart Pattern

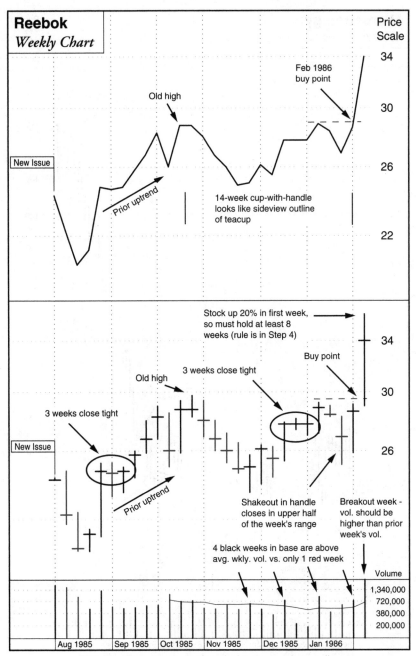

Reebok
Weekly Chart

Price Scale

New Issue

Old high

Feb 1986
buy point

34

30

26

22

Prior uptrend

14-week cup-with-handle
looks like sideview outline
of teacup

Stock up 20% in first week,
so must hold at least 8
weeks (rule is in Step 4)

34

Buy point

3 weeks close tight

Old high

30

3 weeks close tight

New Issue

26

Prior uptrend

Shakeout in handle
closes in upper half
of the week's range

Breakout week -
vol. should be
higher than prior
week's vol.

4 black weeks in base are above
avg. wkly. vol. vs. only 1 red week

Volume

1,340,000
720,000
380,000
200,000

| Aug 1985 | Sep 1985 | Oct 1985 | Nov 1985 | Dec 1985 | Jan 1986 |

Weekly Chart Version of Reebok's Cup-with-Handle

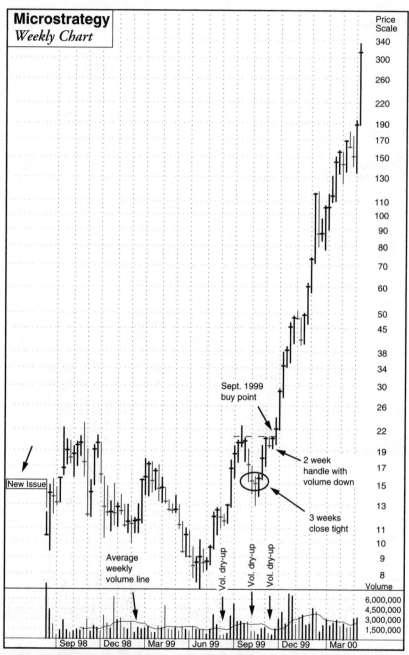

Microstrategy
Weekly Chart

Price Scale

New Issue

Sept. 1999
buy point

2 week
handle with
volume down

3 weeks
close tight

Average
weekly
volume line

Vol. dry-up

Vol. dry-up

Vol. dry-up

Volume

340
300
260
220
190
170
150
130
110
100
90
80
70
60
50
45
38
34
30
26
22
19
17
15
13
11
10
9
8

6,000,000
4,500,000
3,000,000
1,500,000

Sep 98   Dec 98   Mar 99   Jun 99   Sep 99   Dec 99   Mar 00

Eight-Week Cup-with-Handle up 1,414 Percent in Only 24 Weeks

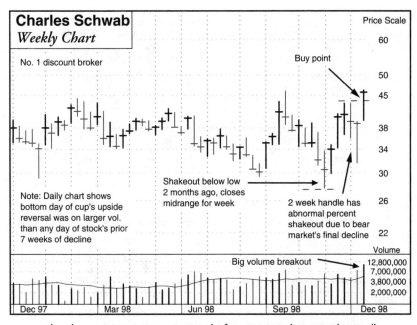

Charles Schwab
Weekly Chart

No. 1 discount broker

Buy point

Price Scale
60
50
45
38
34
30

Shakeout below low
2 months ago, closes
midrange for week

Note: Daily chart shows
bottom day of cup's upside
reversal was on larger vol.
than any day of stock's prior
7 weeks of decline

2 week handle has
abnormal percent
shakeout due to bear
market's final decline

26

22

Volume

Big volume breakout

12,800,000
7,000,000
3,800,000
2,000,000

Dec 97   Mar 98   Jun 98   Sep 98   Dec 98

Schwab up 428 Percent in 26 Weeks from 12-Week Cup-with-Handle

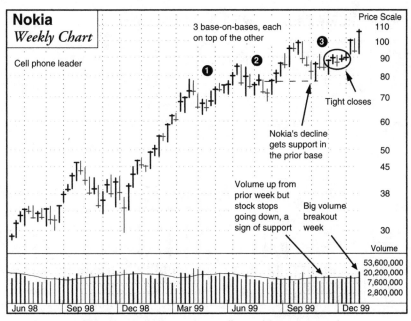

Nokia
Weekly Chart

Cell phone leader

3 base-on-bases, each
on top of the other

Price Scale
110
100
90
80
70
60
50
45
38
30

Tight closes

Nokia's decline
gets support in
the prior base

Volume up from
prior week but
stock stops
going down, a
sign of support

Big volume
breakout
week

Volume

53,600,000
20,200,000
7,600,000
2,800,000

Jun 98   Sep 98   Dec 98   Mar 99   Jun 99   Sep 99   Dec 99

Nokia's 13-Week Cup-with-Handle Doubles in 19 Weeks

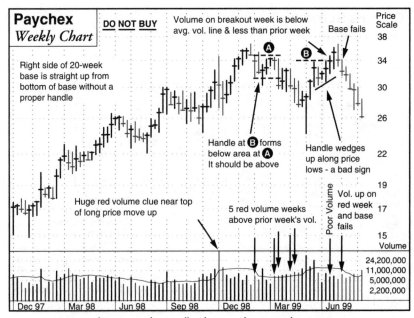

Paychex
Weekly Chart

DO NOT BUY

Volume on breakout week is below avg. vol. line & less than prior week

Base fails

Price Scale
38
34

Right side of 20-week base is straight up from bottom of base without a proper handle

30

26

Handle at **B** forms below area at **A** It should be above

Handle wedges up along price lows - a bad sign

22

19

Huge red volume clue near top of long price move up

5 red volume weeks above prior week's vol.

Poor Volume

Vol. up on red week and base fails

17

15
Volume

24,200,000
11,000,000
5,000,000
2,200,000

| Dec 97 | Mar 98 | Jun 98 | Sep 98 | Dec 98 | Mar 99 | Jun 99 |

Faulty Cup-with-Handle That Wedges up Along Lows

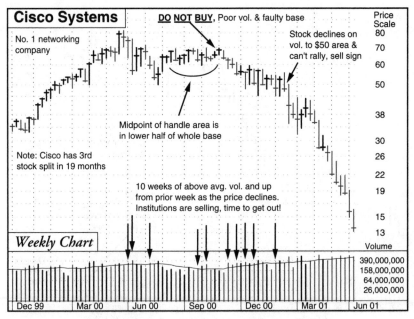

Cisco Systems

DO NOT BUY, Poor vol. & faulty base

Price Scale
80

No. 1 networking company

Stock declines on vol. to $50 area & can't rally, sell sign

70
60
50

Midpoint of handle area is in lower half of whole base

38
30

Note: Cisco has 3rd stock split in 19 months

26
22

10 weeks of above avg. vol. and up from prior week as the price declines. Institutions are selling, time to get out!

19
15

Weekly Chart

13
Volume

390,000,000
158,000,000
64,000,000
26,000,000

| Dec 99 | Mar 00 | Jun 00 | Sep 00 | Dec 00 | Mar 01 | Jun 01 |

Third-Stage Faulty 23-Week Cup-with-Handle Fails

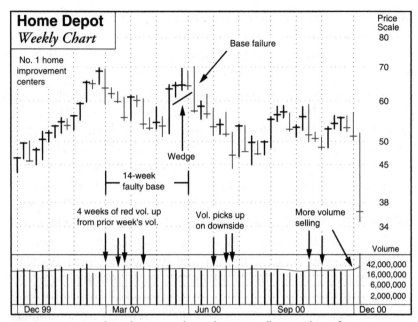

Fourteen-Week Faulty Cup-with-Wedging-Handle Straight up from Lows

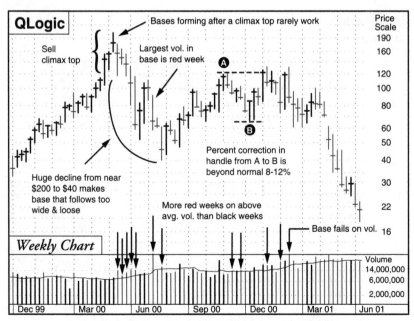

Wide and Loose, Faulty, 39-Week Cup-with-Handle

Many will take six months or a year to form. The correction from the absolute top of the formation to the absolute bottom is generally 25 to 40 percent. Usually the pattern shouldn't correct by more than 2½ times the correction in the overall market averages.

Almost all patterns are built because of a correction, or decline, in the general market indexes. In a sense, market corrections can be viewed as healthy for the future, because they're building the new patterns from which leading stocks can emerge refreshed a few months later. But you've got to stay awake to recognize them. Retail stocks, for example, may be poor choices at one point, but several weeks later can suddenly complete sound patterns and blossom into leaders. To capitalize, however, you need to be there, seeing the change when it happens. It's like anything else: you're either on top of your job or you're not.

Today it's easy to keep up with your investments, even if you're busy working all day. *e*IBD™, a complete electronic version of the printed IBD, is now available anywhere in the world a few hours after the market closes. And on the Web site investors.com, subscribers have free access to professional daily or weekly price and volume

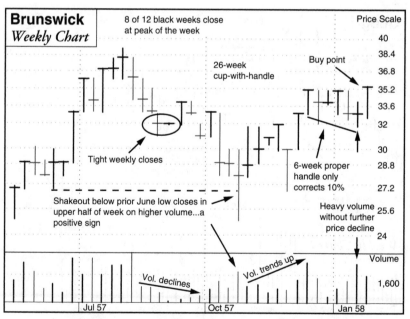

Brunswick Advances 1,605 Percent from This 1958 Cup-with-Handle

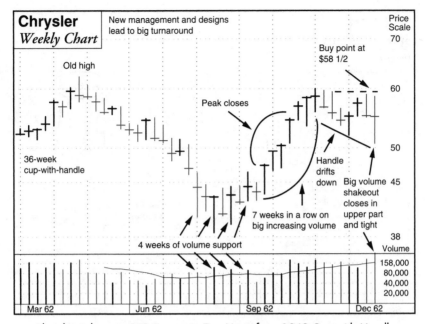

Chrysler Advances 353 Percent in Two Years from 1962 Cup-with-Handle

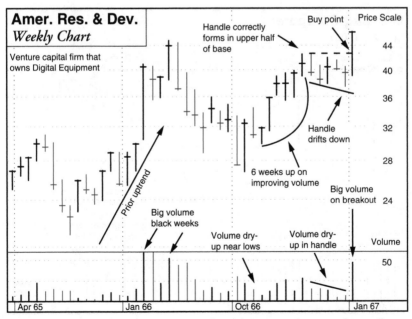

American Res. Increases 830 Percent from This 22-Week Cup-with-Handle

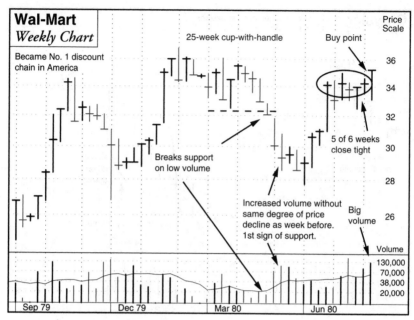

Wal-Mart Cup-with-Handle Increases 957 Percent in Next 36 Months

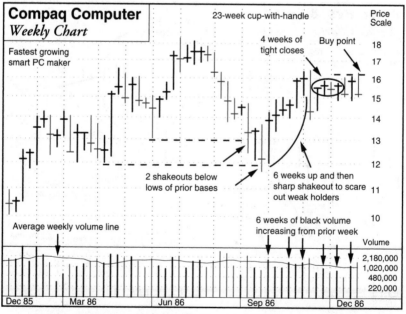

Compaq's 1986 Cup-with-Handle Goes up 378 Percent in 11 Months

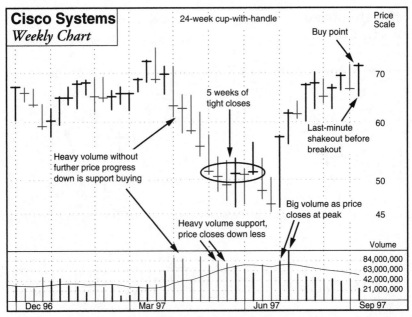

Cisco's 1997 Cup-with-Handle Results in 900 Percent Gain by March 2000

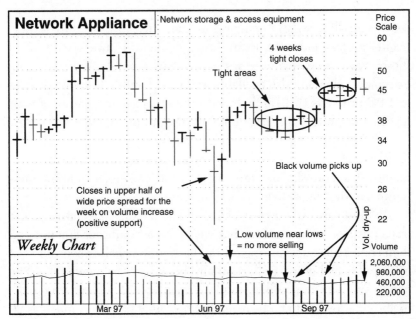

This 1997 Cup-with-Handle Produced over 3700% in 30 Months

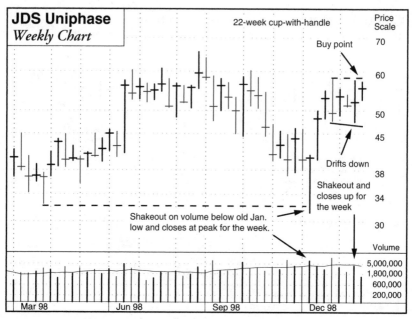

JDS Uniphase
Weekly Chart

22-week cup-with-handle

Price Scale

Buy point

70

60

50

45

Drifts down

38

Shakeout and closes up for the week

34

Shakeout on volume below old Jan. low and closes at peak for the week.

30

Volume

5,000,000
1,800,000
600,000
200,000

Mar 98   Jun 98   Sep 98   Dec 98

Here's a 1998 Cup-with-Handle That Jumped 2016 Percent in 68 Weeks

charts and all past IBD company articles. Just to make sure I thoroughly understand a company fundamentally, I always read all of these previous company stories before I buy any stock. I find them extremely valuable. Also available are many hand-held quote devices and PC products that can help with the efficient monitoring of your investments during the day, in the evening, or on weekends.

Saucer.   This is similar to the cup with a handle, but not seen as frequently. It's more shallow in the depth of its correction, and the minimum length is more than six or eight weeks.

   In most cases you do see a handle. The handle on a cup or saucer has a purpose. When a stock has corrected a significant amount and then comes back up, rallying off the bottom, it usually needs one last price pullback before it takes off and breaks toward new highs. The handle pullback normally is no more than 8 to 12 percent from peak to absolute low. But at a bear market bottom it can be as much as 20 to 30 percent.

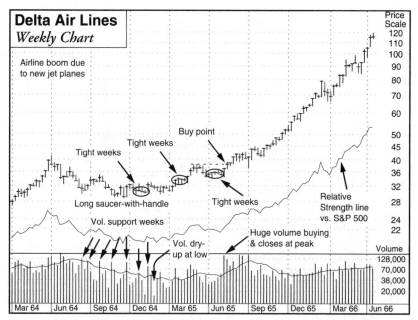

Delta Air Lines
Weekly Chart

Airline boom due to new jet planes

Buy point

Tight weeks

Tight weeks

Long saucer-with-handle

Tight weeks

Vol. support weeks

Relative Strength line vs. S&P 500

Vol. dry-up at low

Huge volume buying & closes at peak

Price Scale
120
110
100
90
80
70
60
50
45
40
36
32
28
24
22

Volume
128,000
70,000
38,000
20,000

Mar 64 | Jun 64 | Sep 64 | Dec 64 | Mar 65 | Jun 65 | Sep 65 | Dec 65 | Mar 66 | Jun 66

Delta's 1965 Saucer-with-Handle Advances 211 Percent in 49 Weeks

The pullback is the stock's one last chance to (1) shake out a few more holders on a day when the market indexes sell off sharply and (2) see if the initial power off the bottom of the whole pattern can retain a significant amount of its move up.

It's no coincidence that many of these corrections and price consolidations that form chart base patterns last 12 or 13 weeks or even 24 to 26 weeks. This corresponds to the three-month cycle in which earnings are reported and shows that many professionals may wait for another earnings report to come out before they commit their funds.

Double bottom. This pattern doesn't occur as frequently as the cup with a handle. It looks like the letter W, but in almost all cases, the second leg down should undercut the low price of the first. This shakes out all the weak holders who didn't get shaken out on the first leg down, and who hoped the decline would stop where it stopped before. Dropping to the lower price may also bring in certain institutional buyers who feel the stock has fallen to a level where they want to buy it. The double bot-

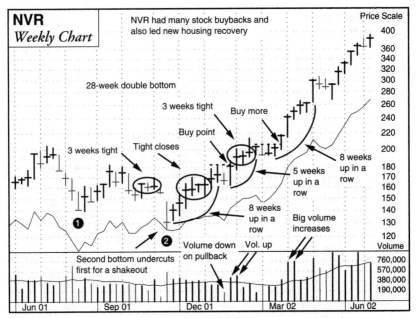

NVR's Double Bottom Moves up 100 Percent in 23 Weeks

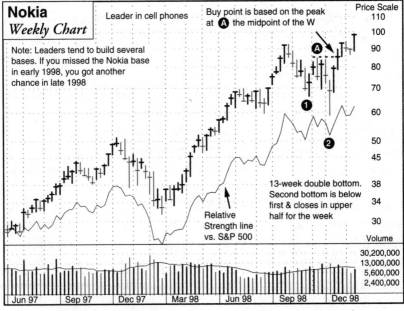

Nokia's 1998 Double Bottom Goes up 450 Percent in 15 Months

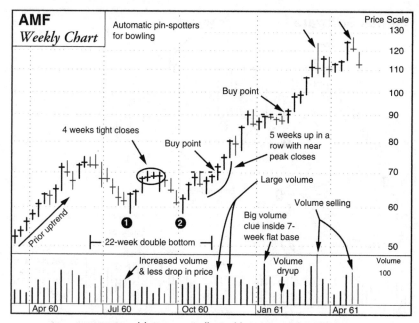

Here's AMF's Double Bottom Followed by a Seven-Week Flat Base

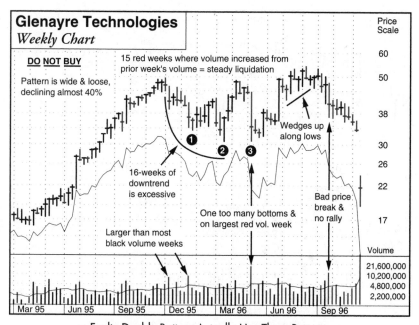

Faulty Double Bottom Actually Has Three Bottoms

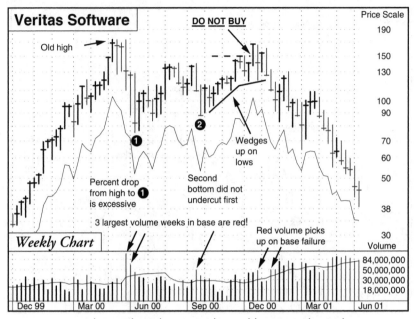

Another Wide and Loose Faulty Double Bottom That Fails

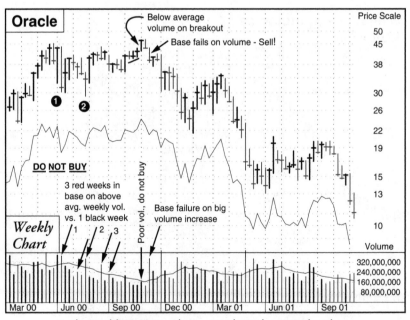

Faulty Double Bottom with More Red Weeks on High Volume

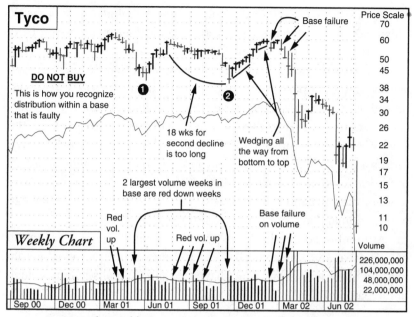

Tyco's Faulty Double Bottom's Two Largest-Volume Weeks Are Red

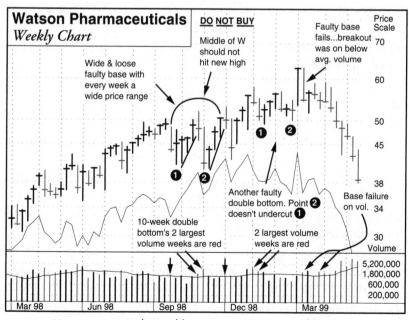

Here Are Two Faulty Double Bottoms, One on Top of the Other

tom's pivot, or exact buy price, is the same as the middle peak in the W. This peak should definitely be below the old high peak price of the overall double-bottom pattern.

When stocks break out of these bases, insist that the day's trading volume be up 50 percent or more from its daily average. Great winners of the past have shown volume increases of 100, 200, or 300 percent or more on the days they charged through their buy points. If the stock's volume was up only 25 percent or less on the breakout day, there's a fair chance it may fail because there's not enough informed professional demand at a key point. If the weekly chart shows less volume for the breakout week than the week before, this is another sign of poor demand at a critical time and potential failure.

As mentioned, the best buy point is usually the peak price in the handle area, and this could be 5 to 15 percent below the actual old high. In other words, you don't have to wait for an absolute new high in the pattern.

Flat base.   This chart pattern goes more or less straight sideways, not correcting too much (10 to 15 percent). It usually forms as a second-stage base after a stock has advanced and retained most of the 20 to 25 percent or more move from its initial base. Its time parameter can be shorter—five or six weeks versus a minimum of seven or eight weeks or more in the other patterns.

Ascending base.   This pattern is another base that occurs after a stock has broken out of an initial cup-with-a-handle or double-bottom pattern and run up partway through its overall rise. It's generally 9 to 16 weeks in duration, with three 10 to 20 percent pullbacks in price. Each pullback low ends at a slightly higher price level, and each rally goes a little bit into new highs. That's why we've labeled it an ascending base. Short-term general market sell-offs are almost always the cause of these three price pullbacks.

When analyzing patterns in weekly charts, you can go week by week, taking note of both the price and volume action for each week. The pattern begins with the first week closing down from the stock's peak week, right on through to the pivot, or classic buying point. After a while, you'll be able to differentiate normal or positive action from

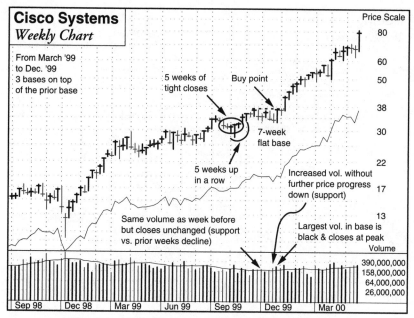

Cisco Systems
Weekly Chart

From March '99
to Dec. '99
3 bases on top
of the prior base

5 weeks of
tight closes

Buy point

7-week
flat base

5 weeks up
in a row

Increased vol. without
further price progress
down (support)

Same volume as week before
but closes unchanged (support
vs. prior weeks decline)

Largest vol. in base is
black & closes at peak

Price Scale
80
60
50
38
30
22
17
13
Volume

390,000,000
158,000,000
64,000,000
26,000,000

Sep 98 Dec 98 Mar 99 Jun 99 Sep 99 Dec 99 Mar 00

Cisco's Last Good Base . . . a Flat Base on Top of a Base

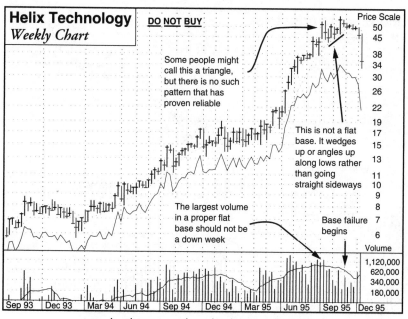

Helix Technology
Weekly Chart

DO NOT BUY

Some people might
call this a triangle,
but there is no such
pattern that has
proven reliable

This is not a flat
base. It wedges
up or angles up
along lows rather
than going
straight sideways

The largest volume
in a proper flat
base should not be
a down week

Base failure
begins

Price Scale
50
45
38
34
30
26
22
19
17
15
13
11
10
9
8
7
6
Volume

1,120,000
620,000
340,000
180,000

Sep 93 Dec 93 Mar 94 Jun 94 Sep 94 Dec 94 Mar 95 Jun 95 Sep 95 Dec 95

A Faulty Flat Base with Bad Volume and Wedging

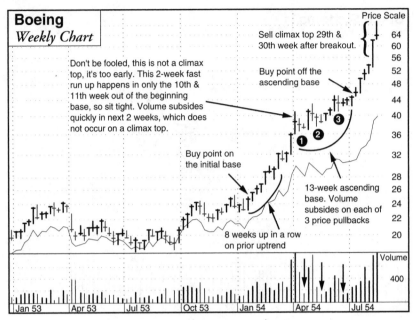

Boeing's 13-Week 1954 Ascending Base

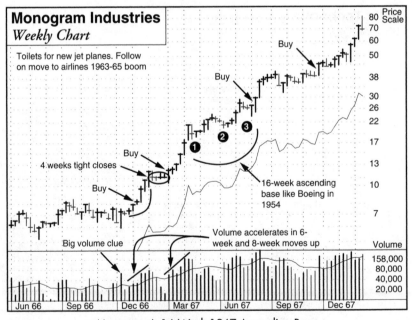

Monogram's 16-Week 1967 Ascending Base

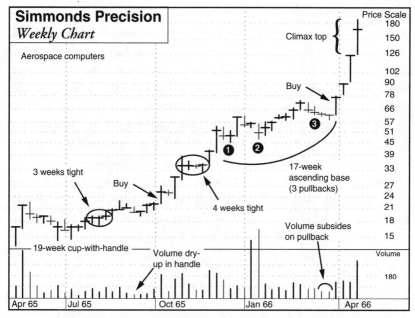

Simmond's 1966 17-Week Version of an Ascending Base

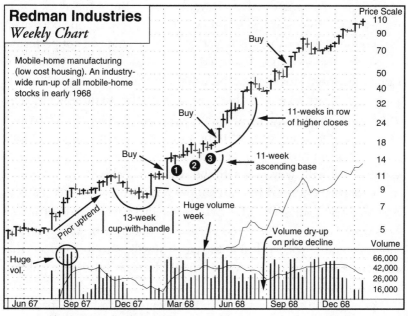

Redman Overall 900 Percent Move Shows an Early Ascending Base

abnormal or negative action. It's normal, for example, for volume to pick up in a week or two as the stock works its way down the left side of the cup. But in most cases you shouldn't see five or six weeks of heavy volume on down weeks. That indicates more selling than is normal, which lowers the odds that the stock will be able to emerge successfully from the base.

To help you spot abnormal volume more easily, we draw a line through the weekly volume plot at the bottom of the charts we produce that indicates average weekly volume over the last three months. You can then count the number of weeks a stock closed down in price from the prior week on greater than average volume. Start from the beginning of the base (the first week that closes down) to the completion of the handle just before the stock breaks out. Then compare that number to the number of weeks that closed on above average volume with the price being up.

The majority of strong, healthy stocks that haven't suffered too much distribution or professional selling should show more weeks up on greater than average volume than weeks down on greater than average volume. An outstanding stock might show eight weeks up on above average weekly volume and only four weeks down. But if the stock you're interested in shows seven weeks down and only four up on above average volume, the probability is high that it's faulty and will not perform.

This is just one of the informed advantages you will have over the average investor, stockbroker, or academic who never takes the time to check or learn to read a chart properly or, due to disbelief or pure ignorance, doesn't understand how important it is to be able to spot volume accumulation or distribution in a stock chart pattern. Again, you could liken this to a doctor never taking blood tests or x-rays to see what's actually going on with the patient's health.

Now you've moved beyond simple recognition of stock patterns by shape. You're dissecting the patterns week by week to determine if the stock's correction has been normal and healthy or abnormal and faulty. The more you work at it, the easier it will be to spot defects that will save you costly mistakes. This should be worth thousands of dollars to you in the future.

A defect you should learn to spot in a cup-with-a-handle pattern is a handle that drifts up rather than down along its low prices. We call this wedging up. A few patterns with wedging handles work, but most fail. The purpose of a downward correction in the lower part of the handle is to put holders through one last decline and shakeout as well as to have a normal correction and pullback in price after the initial strong move up off the bottom of the cup into the upper half of the whole chart pattern.

Sometimes the handle will correct sharply, or shake out, in its first week or two. But usually it shakes out near the end. Once that has occurred at the end of a handle, and the stock turns and runs up through its pivot price on increasing volume, it's usually the perfect time to buy when you're in a bull market. Some investors use a ruler to draw a downward-sloping trend line from the absolute peak at the beginning of the overall pattern that then touches the peak at the beginning of the handle and goes on to establish a slightly earlier starting point just prior to the pivot breakout price. Other professional money managers may start their buying even earlier—around the bottom pullback point of the handle when volume has subsided dramatically. The handle area can be short, going sideways for only 1 or 2 weeks, or it can be longer, taking up to 10 weeks or so. A few cups do not have any handle.

Also beware of handles that form in the lower half of the overall pattern. To determine if that is the case, take the absolute peak of the stock and the absolute low of the pattern and then determine where the midpoint of the handle is in relation to them. If the midpoint of the handle is in the lower half of that entire price structure, it's a weaker pattern prone to failure. The stock didn't lift far enough off the absolute lows of the base pattern to show real power. You want to develop over time the ability to recognize weakness versus strength and power in your stocks' behavior.

A handle can also be too wide and loose pricewise. If you're in a bull market, the handle shouldn't normally correct more than 10 to 15 percent from its absolute peak to its absolute low. But if you're just emerging out of a bear market, the excessive final decline and volatility in the general market can frequently justify a wider handle of 20 to 30 percent. This occurred in Charles Schwab stock in October 1998, before it advanced 428 percent in only 26 weeks.

An entire base structure can be wide and loose too. There are three ways to determine this. We've already noted that the correction in a stock should be no more than 2½ times the correction in the general market index. You can also measure a correction from the absolute peak of a pattern to the absolute low. A correction of 60 percent is usually too wide: the stock simply came down and went up too much. A better-contained 25 to 35 percent correction is more normal in bull markets.

A third way to determine whether the base is too wide and loose is by looking at the spread between the absolute peak and the absolute low of each week's price movement. An example would be a stock that corrects overall from 50 to 30 and the very first week drops to 42 (an 8-point spread), then rallies up 7 the next week only to drop 9 the week after that. If such big swings persist every week throughout the entire base, the stock is too active and erratic. It never has a chance to rest, and it's in the public's eye too much. It calls too much attention to itself. A correction should take some attention away from the stock at some point.

Normal patterns, in fact, will have weeks in which there isn't much trading action at all. These will show up as small, tight movements. For example, a stock might move up from the bottom of a cup at 40 to about 46. Then, around the 46 area, it might go sideways between 45 and 46½ for three weeks and close essentially unchanged every week. The stock isn't being noticed because it isn't doing a lot. But it may be just playing possum. You'll often see this near the end of handles. Trading volume will dry up with tiny price movement and then, when no one's paying attention, it'll take on a whole new personality and suddenly shoot up on huge volume.

This can also happen in a few outstanding new leaders two to four weeks after they break out of proper bases. Funds may still be accumulating a position, and the stock will close three weeks in a row in a tight range substantially unchanged. A few historical examples are Simmonds Precision Products in November 1965, Monogram Industries in December 1966, Home Depot in March 1982 (shortly after its IPO), Emulex in September 1982, Amgen in March 1990, Micron Technology in January 1995, and Oracle in October 1999.

Patterns that are obvious to everyone simply don't work well. They need to be not so obvious to most investors. Remember: the market moves opposite to majority or crowd consensus thinking.

Tightness in a chart pattern is always worth noting: it indicates that an institution or professional could be acquiring a quantity of the stock in a certain price zone over a period of several weeks.

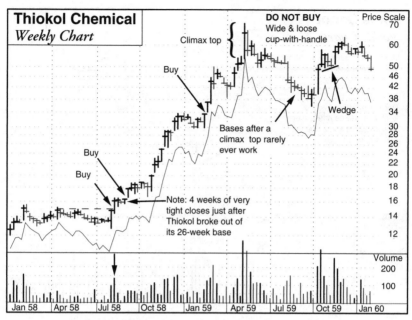

Thiokol in 1958 Has Four Weeks Tight After Breaking Out

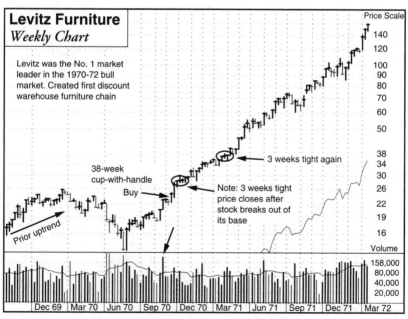

Levitz Furniture in 1970 Has Three Weeks Tight After Breaking Out

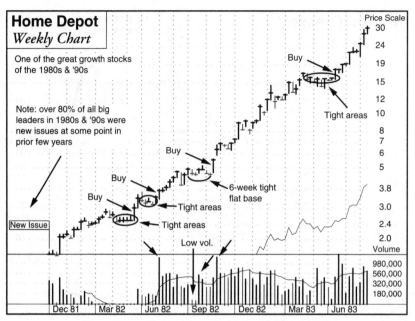

Home Depot
Weekly Chart

One of the great growth stocks of the 1980s & '90s

Note: over 80% of all big leaders in 1980s & '90s were new issues at some point in prior few years

New Issue

Buy

Buy

Buy

Tight areas

Tight areas

6-week tight flat base

Low vol.

Buy

Tight areas

Price Scale
30
24
19
15
12
10
8
7
6
5
3.8
3.0
2.4
2.0
Volume
980,000
560,000
320,000
180,000

Dec 81 | Mar 82 | Jun 82 | Sep 82 | Dec 82 | Mar 83 | Jun 83

Home Depot Shows Many Tight Areas After Its IPO

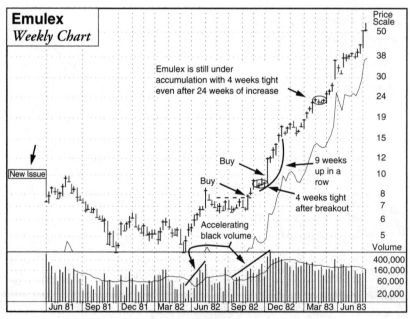

Emulex
Weekly Chart

Emulex is still under accumulation with 4 weeks tight even after 24 weeks of increase

New Issue

Buy

Buy

9 weeks up in a row

4 weeks tight after breakout

Accelerating black volume

Price Scale
50
38
30
24
19
15
12
10
8
7
6
5
Volume
400,000
160,000
60,000
20,000

Jun 81 | Sep 81 | Dec 81 | Mar 82 | Jun 82 | Sep 82 | Dec 82 | Mar 83 | Jun 83

Emulex in 1982 Has Four Weeks Tight After Breakout

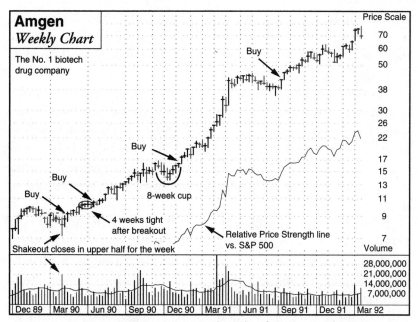

Amgen in 1990 Has Four Weeks Tight After Base Breakout

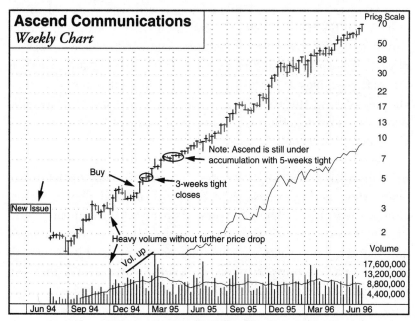

Ascend in 1995 Has Five Weeks Tight After a Large Price Increase

Double-bottom patterns can also have faulty characteristics. It's not sound in the majority of cases, for example, if the middle part of the W goes into new high ground. A proper-looking W has the middle part stopping before the old high.

It's not important to understand what's causing a pattern to look a certain way or why a stock is strong one day and weak another. In many cases, you simply aren't going to know. And even when you think you know, it may be something else entirely. The only thing that's important is that you recognize whether a pattern is strong or weak, normal or abnormal. You'll never know all the answers, and it's not worth trying to find them out.

Sometimes a stock will weaken simply because the general market is breaking down for two or three days in reaction to some temporary bad news. At that point, a stock that's made a cup with a handle might undercut the low in its handle and create a big shakeout. But if the market turns back up a few days later, and if the stock has some real sponsorship, it'll come out of the pattern and break to new high ground on big volume.

Most investors have never studied charts. Of the few who have, many may think it's some kind of Ouija-board-type technical witchcraft. What the masses believe about the market, however, is usually completely off. Naturally, something that works well wouldn't be obvious to everybody, and competent, experienced chart analysis is one of those things. It's a skill, and like all skills it takes a little practice and persistence. But it's well worth learning. The fact is, those who don't use charts together with fundamental research are at a serious disadvantage and could lose a lot of money.

Most professional investors—or at least the very best ones—carefully analyze the supply and demand patterns and characteristics charts show and then base their decisions on what they're seeing, along with what they know fundamentally about the company. Most high-performance professionals always use both strong fundamentals and market action facts, not just one or the other. Fundamentals alone also can't in most cases tell you when a market leader tops, but observation of a stock's abnormal price and volume activity can.

When to Sell and Nail Down Your Big Profit While You Still Have It

Now that you know how to tell which way the general market is going, how to execute the 3-to-1 profit-and-loss plan, and how to select and buy the very best stocks at exactly the right time, you're more than halfway to becoming a far more successful investor. However, having a paper profit in a stock is one thing; keeping it is another. I know. I learned the hard way more than 40 years ago, in the bull market of 1961.

I owned a half dozen stocks that turned out to be big winners. They included Kerr McGee Oil, an oil and uranium producer founded by former Oklahoma governor Bob Kerr and oilman Dean McGee; Crown Cork & Seal, a developer of aerosol cans; and Brunswick Corp. and American Machine & Foundry (AMF), both of which set off a bowling craze by creating automatic pinsetters. Because I had pyramided, or added to my holdings as they advanced, there were good positions in each. But then they topped and came down enough that I lost all of the gains that had been achieved.

Fortunately, I started to sell and got out before being seriously hurt. But after being dead right on both the market and my stocks, I was so upset about finishing only even that year that I sat down and tried to figure out where I had gone wrong. I still wasn't making any money, just spinning my wheels.

That was when I finally discovered the brutal truth: I didn't have a clue about when to sell a stock. I was just buying stocks because they were great, and adding to them because they were working, and then sitting back—fat, dumb, and happy. I had no realistic understanding that most market leaders will at some point top, come back down, and wipe out most of your profits before you know what hit you.

It was then that I discovered, through weeks of self-analysis of all of my mistakes and detailed research, that many stocks coming out of proper bases would go up about 20 to 25 percent, correct, and then— if they were still sound—build another base and go up another 25 or 30 percent. That's when I came up with the rule to take many of my gains when they were up 20 or 25 percent, while they were still advancing, and cut all losses at 7 or 8 percent.

When you go through a complete market cycle—from the start of a new bull to the bottom of the next bear—your real objective is to nail down as much of the profits you've built as possible. Most investors, however, give back more of their profits than they should, and too many give back the whole thing and then some. If you read this chapter several times, you should be able to skillfully execute historically proven sell rules and not give back most of your profits in future bull markets. You positively must learn and profit from all of your past market mistakes.

The only way I know to nail down a profit is to sell on the way up, when your stock is still advancing and in good health. As we demonstrated in Chapter 2, you can do well if you take many of your profits on the way up at 20 or 25 percent and cut all your losses at 7 or 8 percent. Under this system, you will sooner or later put together two or three 25 percent gains in a row. Three 25 percent gains in a row will nearly double your money (or triple it if you're fully margined).

Notice I say take *many* profits at 20 to 25 percent. There's a key exception to the rule that I always apply to this very day. If it's a strong bull market, and if a stock I just bought has great current and three-year earnings and sales growth, a high ROE, and better-quality sponsorship and is a leader in a strong industry group, and if it bolts 20 percent on good volume in just one, two, or three weeks when it breaks out of a sound and proper base, I set it aside and must hold it for at least eight weeks from its breakout buy point.

Our historical studies show that stocks with that much initial rocket-like thrust have the potential to be the biggest winners of all. Not only will they stay out of trouble during those eight weeks, they will probably be ahead more than 20 or 25 percent when the eight weeks are up—and sometimes as much as 50, 60, or even 80 percent.

At that point, you review the situation and decide if your stock should be held still longer for an even bigger gain. To stay with it further, however, you'll need some additional rules or principles based on real market history of past outstanding leaders to guide you. You might decide, for example, that you'll hold the stock for another two months, or through its first 15 to 20 percent correction, or as long as the price stays above or is supported at or slightly below its 10-week moving average price line—anything that lets you get most of the further big move that's there. Or maybe you set a target price objective based on the PE ratio expansion expected from the breakout point of the beginning base and the future earnings estimate, a year or two out. This has helped me very much in being able to sit with most of my big winners long enough to achieve the potential that was there but still get out when the end was near. As Jesse Livermore said, it's your sitting, not your thinking, that makes the big money for you.

If you collect and keep your old charts of former big leaders from earlier cycles, you might even find a past winner that behaved in a similar manner to your current stock and use that as a precedent or guide to help you hang in there with your stock as long as its price corrections are normal. I did this very thing when I bought America Online at 60 in the last week of October 1998. The stock broke out of a cup-with-a-handle pattern and afterward was up 25 percent in only three weeks. The Dow had just had its follow-through day, confirming the beginning of a new uptrending market, and AOL acted like it could be the leader of the general market turnaround.

Thirty-three years earlier, in July 1965, I had bought Fairchild Camera and Instrument, a semiconductor leader that was benefiting from the demand for electronics during the Vietnam War. I got it at 50 when it broke out of a cup-with-no-handle pattern just after the market also had a big follow-through day. Fairchild initially ran up 25 percent in the first three weeks and 50 percent in its first five weeks. It then broke badly for one week on huge volume, creating a scary shakeout. Next it proceeded to triple from $70 to $215 a share in the following six months.

This is exactly what America Online did. It raced up 25 percent in only three weeks and 50 percent in its first five weeks. But then it broke badly for one week on terrific scare-type volume. Because I had the old Fairchild chart as a precedent, I wasn't shaken out on AOL's heavy-volume break, which really was a normal occurrence historically. AOL quickly recovered and more than tripled in price from there. I finally sold it when it ended its more than 450 percent runup with a climax top in early April 1999. You can always learn from history, because human nature doesn't change and there's really not as much that's new in the market as most people believe.

The last leg of AOL's tremendous run emerged from a nine-week ascending base nearly identical to earlier ascending bases of aerospace giant Boeing in the second quarter of 1954 and Redman Industries in the big mobile home move that began in the first quarter of 1968. Back then, I was shaken out of Redman during an intermediate-term (8 to 10 percent) general market correction in that first quarter of 1968 only to see it later increase 670 percent. I well remember that extremely expensive lesson and, as a result, sat through the three pullbacks in AOL's ascending base. You can compare AOL's chart with the Redman and Boeing ascending base precedents in the last part of the previous chapter.

AOL's climax run, moreover, was textbook—exactly like previous climax tops described in detail in my first and second editions of *How To Make Money in Stocks.* It nearly doubled in just five weeks out of the ascending base, had an exhaustion gap two days from the top, and on the next to last day surged 16 points.

AOL was bought strictly according to the rules, held according to the rules, and sold on the way up while it was still advancing according to the rules—no personal opinions. The price-to-earnings ratio when AOL was bought at the beginning buy point was 158. At the stock's peak, it was 532. I learned a long time ago by analyzing all big winners historically that a stock's PE ratio is simply not a cause of performance, but the end effect of the true cause of performance—a stock's outstanding earnings performance and institutional sponsorship. Most media journalists, analysts, and value investors miss the

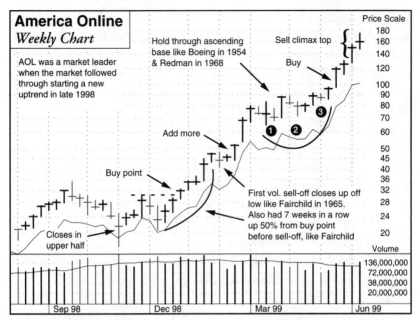

AOL Follows 1965 Fairchild and 1954 Boeing Precedents

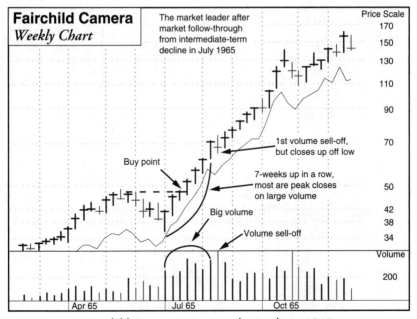

Fairchild Camera Is No. 1 Market Leader in 1965

really great companies because they don't understand you can't buy a Mercedes for the price of a Chevrolet. Stocks are like professional athletes. The best ones are always higher priced.

Making the crucial exception to the "sell when you're up 20 to 25 percent" rule will let you have, in addition to your many singles and doubles, a home run now and then in which a CAN SLIM stock will go up 100 or 200 percent or even more. So, if your stock is clearly one of the market's very best performers, you might try to sit with it until it has a chance to make a climax top. This is the way four of every five big leaders usually end up.

During a climax top, a stock leader that has risen for many months will suddenly take off and run up much faster than it has in any week since the start of its whole original move. On a weekly chart, the spread from the absolute low to the absolute high of the week in almost all examples will be wider than any price spread in any week so far.

If you don't use charts—which in my view is probably a mistake— you can tell a climax top by noting day-to-day price changes. Many will run up 7 or 8 of 10 days in a row and one of those days will show

Amazon Makes a Classic Climax Top and Then Declines 95 Percent

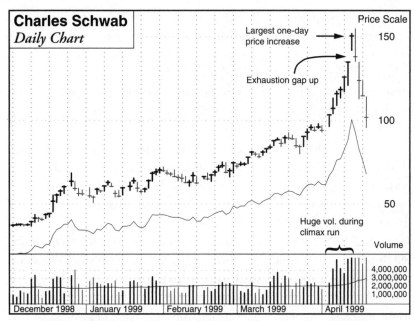

Charles Schwab Also Completes Its Huge Advance with a Climax Top

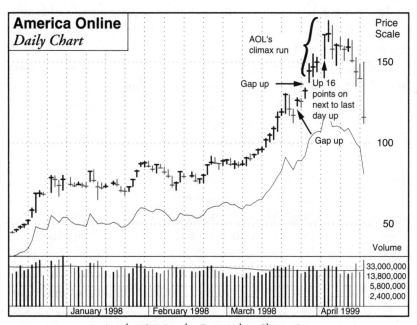

Another Big Leader Tops with a Climax Run

the biggest point gain since the stock broke out of its original base. For example, say a stock that's been moving up for several months, but never by more than 8 points in any one day, shoots up 12 points. When that happens along with the several other characteristics we've mentioned, you know you could be just several days away from the ultimate top. Daily and weekly charts make it very easy to stay on top of and monitor your stocks more effectively.

Some call this pattern a blow-off top, others call it a climax top. Whatever the name, it describes a situation in which seemingly everybody is buying a stock that looks for all the world like it's going to double again. But it's just at that point, when the crowd is all excited and drawn into it, that the bubble will break.

A final telltale sign of a climax top, as mentioned in the AOL example, is when, after months of advancing, a fast-running stock opens on what is called an exhaustion gap. For example, it might close the night before at $70 and open the next morning at $75, without making all the usual stops in between. That's a sign you're at the very end, and you want to be selling. You could be within a day or two of the top.

At such moments, it's important not to hesitate. You want to sell while the stock is still advancing and looks super-powerful, because once it does top, it can break very sharply. In as little as two days, it can retrace much of its final runup.

Pulling the trigger won't be easy. Everyone will be running around saying, "Wow! Look at this stock—it's fantastic!" And it will be fantastic. During its blow-off in late December 1999 and early January 2000, Qualcomm—a cell phone leader that made a 20-fold move in 15 months—rocketed 100 percent, from $100 to $200, in its final three weeks. It too opened on an exhaustion gap and closed up an unbelievable 39 points for that one day, just three days from its top.

Making the sell decision even tougher at times like this will be that several brokerage firms may be recommending the stock as a buy. They too may be so caught up in it, and so impressed with the latest move, that they'll be raising both their earnings estimates and their share price targets. Several well-known Wall Street firms did this when Charles Schwab hit $150 at the top day of its climax run in April 1999. You, however, will know better, especially after you've experienced a climax top or two. You'll know that when everybody's running

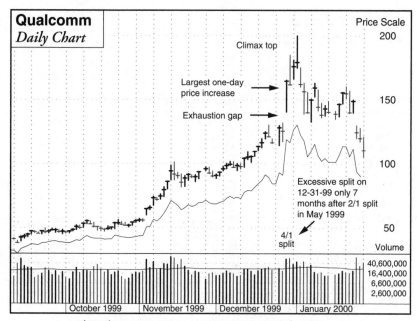

Qualcomm
Daily Chart

Price Scale
200

Climax top

Largest one-day
price increase →

Exhaustion gap →

150

100

Excessive split on
12-31-99 only 7
months after 2/1 split
in May 1999

4/1
split

50

Volume

40,600,000
16,400,000
6,600,000
2,600,000

October 1999 | November 1999 | December 1999 | January 2000

This Climax Top Was up 100 Percent in Only 15 Days

around saying how great a stock is, everybody who can buy probably already has, and the only direction for the stock to go at that point is down. When it's obvious and exciting to everyone, it's too late. Crowd psychology is always wrong at crucial market turning points, when it's most important to be right.

Another way of pegging the possible top in a great stock is by measuring how much its price-to-earnings ratio has expanded. The PE of a leading stock that meets all the growth parameters will expand more than 100 percent from where it was when the stock began its whole move. Say a stock breaks out of a sound first-stage base at $50 and goes to $150. And say the $50 price was 40 times the then current 12-month earnings. If the $150 price is 95 times earnings (or 138 percent the beginning PE of 40), that could be another sign you're living on borrowed time.

These warning signs can be used as a post-eight-week sell rule for that stock you're sticking with for a bigger gain. In some cases, a stock will top with two or more signals being tripped off. You could see a cli-

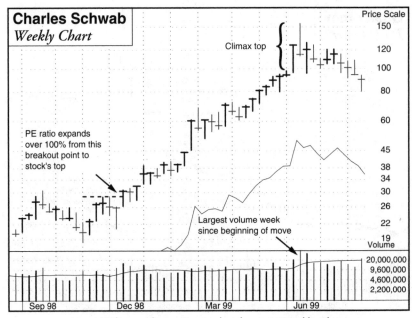

Charles Schwab
Weekly Chart

Climax top

PE ratio expands
over 100% from this
breakout point to
stock's top

Largest volume week
since beginning of move

Price Scale
150
120
100
80
60
45
38
34
30
26
22
19
Volume

20,000,000
9,600,000
4,600,000
2,200,000

Sep 98   Dec 98   Mar 99   Jun 99

Here's What a Climax Top Looks Like on a Weekly Chart

max run and an exhaustion gap, for example, at the same time the PE has gotten to 120 or 130 percent of where it was at the start. This too is what happened to Charles Schwab.

Once you've seen a few of these blow-offs, it's fascinating to watch them occur over and over again. It may be Schwab this time, someone else next time. But in every stock market and economic cycle through the entire twentieth century, the big funds and professional pools went after the best growth stocks at the time, ran them up, and eventually pushed PEs to levels no one could justify. It's just history repeating itself over and over again, human nature continually on parade.

The real question is: are you willing to do the extra study to learn from history? Or is that too much work; does it seem much easier to keep making the same mistake you or your advisor may have made in the past?

Still another way to spot the end of a market leader's long run is to use what we call channel lines. Again using a chart (daily or weekly), draw upward-trending straight lines connecting three major lows along the absolute bottom of a stock's temporary pullbacks in price and then a second line connecting three major highs along the top. Pick points after the stock comes out of its first base and put a little time in between each plot point—a few months rather than a few weeks—so that what you're plotting is the major trend. The lines you draw will not be exactly parallel, but they'll be close.

If a stock goes through an upper channel line—crossing the channel line at 50, for example, and getting as high as 51 or 52—you can sell knowing that 75 to 80 percent of the time you're near a top. All it takes is one penetration, even during intraday trading. Sell the stock as soon as it goes through. Don't wait to see what happens next. But don't jump the gun, either. A stock that's still working its way higher will often not penetrate the upper channel line but bounce off the top trend line back down in price, then turn and weeks later go back up to it again, staying inside the channel all the while.

Another way of knowing when the ice is thinning out under a great stock is by keeping track of the chart bases it forms on the way up. As

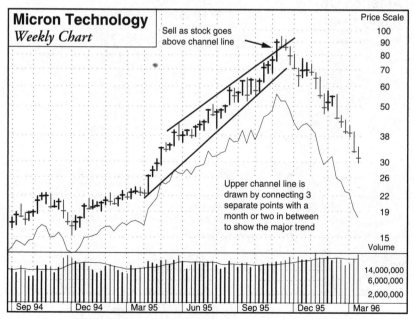

Sell When Stock Goes Above a Major Upper Channel Line

85

we've discussed, a new bull market always produces a few dozen new leaders, the best of which will always have strong prior uptrends before they build their first bases. Then they'll break out of those bases and run up 20 to 25 percent or more before correcting. Then they'll form a second base, break out again, and run up another 20 to 25 percent or sometimes more. Some, if they're still fundamentally healthy, will form a third base and break out from there.

The breakout from the first base, *if properly and correctly formed,* will almost always work in a new bull market, because not everyone will have observed or believed it, so fewer investors will have bought it or even know about the stock. It may be a newer company (an IPO in the past few years). A few more people will see the second base if it's soundly formed, but there are not usually enough buyers to pose a great danger to the breakout. If too many see it, or if its formation is faulty, it could of course fail.

By the time a stock has formed a third base, however, most of the

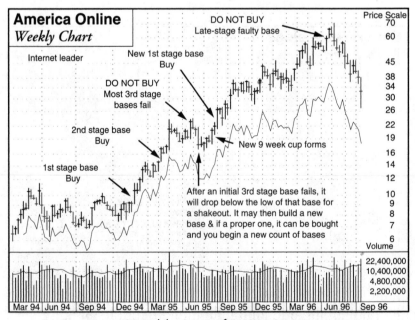

AOL and the Stages of Its Many Bases

smart money will not only know the stock but will have become conditioned to how it acts. Many will own a piece of it, and some—especially those who were in early—will already be thinking of selling to those waiting for the next breakout or move upward.

This potential selling lowers the chances that the breakout from the third base will work. If it does work, however, and the stock goes up and builds a fourth base, watch out! A big percentage of the fourth-stage bases will fail as they try to break out. By then, it's obvious to everybody. And in the stock market, as we've said, what's obvious to the crowd rarely works.

Just think of the disadvantage incurred by investors who never use charts and deride the idea out of a lack of knowledge. They never have a clue as to what stage base they are operating out of or even the fact that stocks have late-stage bases and why it's important to recognize them. That's like taking a long cross-country trip without doing any planning beforehand and not taking a road map or a spare tire or

Gartner Has a Late-Stage, Wide and Loose Faulty Base

a cell phone. That's why we created Daily Graphs® in 1972 and Daily Graphs Online®, online investment research tool, to help investors improve their stock selection and timing decisions.

In sum, if you own a CAN SLIM stock that has based and broken out four times, think about selling it. And if you're thinking about buying a stock that's breaking out of a fourth base, think again. True professionals who spend any time with this method are not going to buy anything coming out of a fourth-stage base. The stock may go up 5 or 10 percent and draw in unaware investors. But then it will break very rapidly, dropping down and undercutting the low of the base so that nearly everyone is shaken out with sharp losses in an abrupt failure.

As you become familiar with how chart bases look, you'll see how each one gets a little wider and looser as a market-leading stock moves up, and how fourth-stage bases can be downright sloppy and have more noticeable faults or defects compared to the original correctly formed base.

Details like this do matter. That's why IBD's most successful subscribers read and reread these materials several times to make sure they develop through repetition the skills to recognize and execute all of these important details. To be an investment winner, you have to prepare yourself to win. Luck has nothing to do with it. You can prepare and learn to win if you are determined and learn from all of your past mistakes. All great investors made mistakes in the beginning.

Still another key indicator to watch as strong stocks try to break out of successive bases is the relative price strength line. When a stock breaks out of a buy point near or into new high ground, the thin wavy line below the chart prices tracks the stock's relative strength (RS) versus the S&P 500. This RS line should break out too. If it doesn't, it should follow very quickly thereafter, thereby confirming the price move. (Frequently, the RS line will break to new highs in advance of the stock itself, which is very positive.) A lagging relative strength line signals weakness and loss of power and leadership. Avoid buying stocks with this flaw. If you already own such a stock, consider whether it should be sold.

If you don't use charts, you can still track the relative strength by the RS rating itself. In *Investor's Business Daily*, RS ratings run from 1 to 99, with 99 being the strongest. An RS of 90 means that a

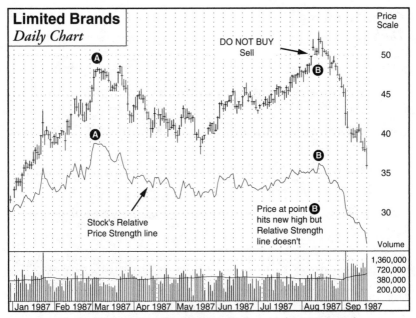

The Limited's Relative Strength Line Fails to Make a New High

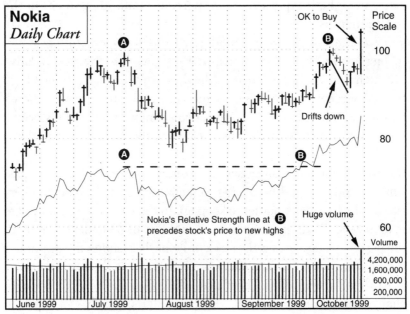

Nokia's Relative Strength Line Hits a New High Before Its Price

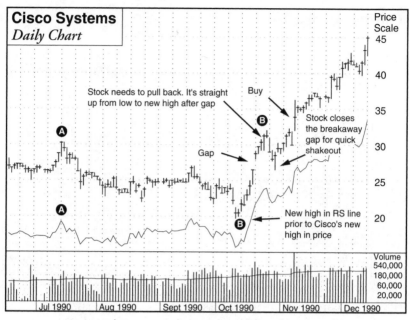

Cisco's Relative Strength Line Hits a High Before the Stock

given stock has outperformed 90 percent of all other stocks in the last 12 months.

For the last 50 years, models of the best-performing stocks in our historical database consistently showed an average Relative Strength Rating of 87 *before* these leaders broke out and advanced 100 to 1000 percent or more. It's been the same cycle after cycle. So there's truly important value in studying and knowing your market history.

If the relative strength drops below 70, this is another sign that a stock is beginning to lag the better-performing leaders and an indication that it should in many cases be considered for selling. The one possible exception would be a large-capitalization growth stock, the very size of which makes it harder to keep up. In this case, you might be able to tolerate an RS dropping to the mid-60s. But an RS under 60, even for the big companies, means the stock probably has neither the power nor the earnings momentum to become a real leader in the near future.

Investors who don't keep close watch on the relative strength changes of their stocks, or who don't use charts, usually wind up buying a number of stocks with bad relative strength numbers or sitting with stocks showing poor RS numbers. This leads to either poor performance or excessive losses that otherwise could have been better controlled. There is no reason any investor should ever in any bull market buy or sit with a poor-performing stock with a Relative Strength Rating of 10, 20, 30, 40, or 50. The market is bluntly telling you that investment is a relatively poor or mediocre choice. On average, if your portfolio has a number of stocks like this, you will not likely make significant progress.

You should also know that more than half the leaders in a market cycle will be part of a strong-performing industry group. If you buy a leader in a leading group, keep an eye on the one or two other leaders in the same group. If you own Wal-Mart Stores, for example, you might also watch stocks like Home Depot, Kohl's, and other leading retail chains. If those stocks are making major tops, you've got to ask yourself if yours could possibly be next.

Be just as wary if your stock is the only one in its group that's doing well. You don't want yours to be the one that's holding up when institutional investors are getting after all the others. At some point, the selling can wash over the entire group.

Don't assume that all industry groups are the same, however. In a new bull market, five, six, or seven groups will do well and probably lead. But each will have characteristics of its own. The market may like home builders and be taking up all, or nearly all, of the 25 stocks in that group. Another group might have 10 stocks, but only 2 or 3 might be leading while the rest dog it.

In other words, just because a group is strong doesn't mean all the stocks that comprise it are going up. Always avoid the laggards in the group! Again: keep your eye on the two or three leaders that are doing best. If one key leading stock in the group gets into trouble, carefully watch the remaining leaders in the group.

A stock that goes up substantially will usually split once or twice during a bull cycle. Companies like to split their stock to keep the price attractive to individual investors, among other reasons. After a stock split, there are more shares outstanding, but the market value remains the same.

91

Say you own 200 shares of a stock that's trading at $80 a share—a $16,000 investment—and the company announces a 2-for-1 split. When the split takes effect, you now have 400 shares. But they will trade at $40. The value is the same—$16,000—but the price per share is lower.

Most investors welcome splits. They believe they're getting more for their money. But as the example shows, that's not the case. A split per se is neither a positive or negative development—except, that is, when it is too large or occurs too frequently.

Splits of 3 for 1, 4 for 1, or 5 for 1 are excessive and often could mark the tops of stocks. It makes sense when you think about it. Excessive divisions suggest the stock has already run up a great deal (or it wouldn't be necessary to split it so far), meaning that everybody who is going to buy it probably has. A stock is also vulnerable if it is split two or more times in rapid succession: a 3-for-2 split, for example, followed 8 or 10 months later by a 2-for-1. For instance, Qualcomm had a 4-for-1 split at its climax top split runup in December of 1999. Only eight months earlier, it had been split 2 for 1.

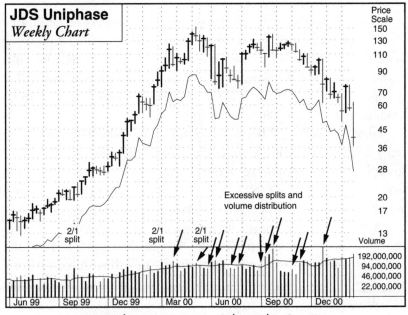

JDS Uniphase Has Excessive Splits Within One Year

This doesn't mean you automatically sell a stock when it has an excessive split. That depends on where the stock is when the split is announced. If it's very extended from its base, it could be vulnerable. But a market-leading stock can also rally on a split, when trading in the new shares begins, and go on to make a climax top.

There's no rule, in other words, that says you should sell a stock just because it has an excessive split. But you need to be aware that numerous stocks could be splitting right around their tops, when everyone sees it and is getting excited. Some professionals will sell right into that situation.

The sell disciplines listed so far are derived from cold, hard technical and fundamental analysis over many years. And you should be just as objective and highly disciplined in applying them. There are a few sell signals, however, that fall into the subjective category. One is when you see a CEO's picture on the cover of *Business Week, Forbes,* or *Fortune,* with a story inside on how great his or her company is. I remember one Internet company in particular a few years ago. You could see by the look on the CEO's face how proud he was of everything he'd accomplished. I remember saying, "It must be all over with now." And sure enough, it was.

Some studies have found that CEOs with huge egos, and especially the hard chargers who lead mainly with their personalities, don't do quite as well in the long run as those with more humility. They also find that the CEOs with the very best records had very few stories written about them while their stocks were making their biggest moves. Wal-Mart had gone up 10 or 20 times before the media really got to know and write about Sam Walton.

Don't worry, then, if the big magazines haven't started writing feature articles about the company you own. The time to worry is when they do. And when they get around to putting a picture of the CEO on the cover, the time may have come to consider selling. Remember: the market is a contrary animal, and when it's finally obvious to the masses, it seldom continues to work. Markets move to fool and outwit the majority.

Also keep an eye out for signs of extravagance—the corporate equivalent of conspicuous consumption. A big new headquarters may be the envy of all the other executives in town, but to you as a shareholder, it could be a sign that the company is starting to splurge and the stock has reached or is nearing a top. Headquarters didn't come any bigger than the Sears Tower in downtown Chicago, started in 1970 and completed in 1973. Sears stock has generally under-performed ever since—for 30 years, to be exact. Tops were also near when the Pan Am building was built over Grand Central Station, when General Motors built executive offices opposite the Plaza Ho-tel, and Gulf + Western built its new headquarters overlooking Central Park, all in New York. Bethlehem Steel's new headquarters building and country club was a similar case, as was the new eToys headquarters on Olympic Boulevard in Los Angeles at the height of the Internet boom.

A warning light should also go on when a company indicates it wants to be the biggest in its field. What usually follows is a merger and acquisition binge that leads to a hangover from which the original company rarely recovers. Does anyone remember the conglomerate craze led by Jimmy Ling? Ling-Temco-Vought sold for $170 in the summer of 1967 when it peaked. Peter Lynch, one of Fidelity Funds' many great portfolio managers, referred to diversification as "de-worseification."

One final tip on selling stocks after a major move up according to time-tested and proven rules, principles, and precedents: when you sell, sell. Don't get cute and unload just a small part of your position. Either you want out or you want in. If you want out, get out.

If you don't sell all your position on the way up, and the stock breaks down, you could start rationalizing. You'll say, "Well, I missed a good chance to take my profit, but now I'll wait until it rallies back." And then it drops some more and you'll say, "Well, I can't sell now because it's down too much." And it drops even more and you'll say, "Well, it was way up here, and now it's way down here. It can't possi-bly go any lower." And you know what happens then.

The only way to avoid that typical psychological trap is to sell on the way up, when you've got a worthwhile gain, and to be happy with the gain. If the stock goes even higher, you've still made your gain and you can take that cash and look for another potential winner. Besides, as we've already noted, if you make three 25 percent profits in a row, you'll be up nearly 100 percent—and that ain't bad. If one of those gains comes from selling into a climax top, your profit may be even bigger.

Also avoid hedging by going long and short at the same time. You may think you're being smart by selling a call option or buying a put, but the person you outsmart may be yourself. You can end up closing out each position at the wrong time and being wrong on both.

Keep it simple. Investing is hard enough. Don't complicate it by getting super-tricky.

STEP 5

Managing Your Portfolio: Time-Proven Methods to Maximize Results and Minimize Losses

Managing a portfolio of stocks is like tending a garden. If you don't keep at it, those lovely flowers you planted will be overrun by unsightly weeds that will give you more headaches than pleasure. The stocks in your portfolio need to be watched just as closely, if not more so. And if weeds appear, don't hesitate to reach for the trowel.

How do you tell the weeds from the flowers? Easy: let the market tell you. The stocks that are up the most from where you bought them are your flowers; those that are down the most, or up the least, are your weeds. If you have five stocks—one up 15 percent, another up 7 percent, one breaking even, one down 5 percent, and another down 10 percent—you start off at the bottom of the pile, with the 10 percent loser.

Sounds simple, but for most investors it isn't. It's only natural to hope that sorry little sprig in the corner of your garden—the one that's struggling to keep up with your other plantings—will sooner or later blossom into a successful investment. But, as we've already learned, the market doesn't care what you hope. Through its auction market pricing action, it's letting you know that one or more of your stocks is deficient. Now it's up to you to accept that reality, act on it, and move on. Only in this way can you keep your portfolio healthy and blooming with winners.

Savvy merchants go about their business in much the same way. If goods aren't moving, they will mark them down so they can sell them quickly and put their money into merchandise more in demand. The "merchandise" you own needs similar supervision. Your list of stocks should be checked every week, every month, every quarter, every year, so that a losing position is never left to languish. You should never, ever have a long-term loss.

Over time, you'll learn that only 1 or 2 of every 10 stocks you buy will be truly outstanding and capable of doubling or tripling or more in value. So it's important to know these when you see them. One way is by carefully watching how a stock performs in its earliest stage. As mentioned in Chapter 3, big potential winners, after breaking out of properly formed bases, will shoot up 20 percent or more in a week or two or three. When that happens in a CAN SLIM stock I've just bought, I will always set it aside mentally and hold it longer. In other words, I will make it the exception to my rule of selling and taking a number of profits at 20 or 25 percent. There's nothing worse than owning stock in the next Microsoft but selling it for a 20 or 30 percent profit and then watching it double or triple afterward. Sold-out bulls are unhappy campers.

Another key to highly successful portfolio management is realizing that your objective in the market isn't just to be right, it's to make big money when you're right. The way you do this is by concentration and judicious, proper follow-up buys rather than broad, unwieldy diversification.

Almost everyone in America today has been brainwashed into believing that wide diversification—spreading your money among many stocks rather than a few—is the secret to safe, prudent investing. But this is only partly true. Yes, the more you diversify, the less risk you have in any one stock. But you're still not protected against substantial losses, and you certainly haven't put yourself in a position to make big money when you're right.

Wide diversification, as far as I'm concerned, is nothing but a hedge against your lack of knowledge. You're not sure what to own, so you buy lots of different equities you don't know quite as much about.

That way, those that go wrong won't hurt you as much as if your portfolio were more concentrated.

If you want to diversify, there's a better-controlled way. Once you decide how much money you have to invest, always put a strict limit on the number of stocks you'll own in your portfolio. Then enforce that limit by refusing to add another stock until you've sold one. If you've decided to own no more than 10 stocks, and you want to make a new purchase, you should force yourself to sell the least attractive of the 10 you've got and use the proceeds for your new buy. If you don't set limits, you'll find that even though you intended to own only 10 stocks, you end up with 15, then 20, then 25. And before you know it, you've got weeds in your flower patch.

No one can fully know and stay on top of several dozen stocks. Over the years, I've found that it's better to put all your eggs in a few baskets and then watch those baskets very closely, knowing what's in them backward and forward.

If I own only four stocks, and the general market starts into an important decline, I probably will have sold one of the four because it triggered a sell rule—like ending in a classic climax top as most leaders did in March 2000, nailing down a 20 to 25 percent gain or cutting short a loss. Another may have been sold because I didn't like the way the general market was acting—for example, showing too many volume distribution days. Already I'd be 50 percent in cash—well on my way to protecting myself by taking out insurance against the possibility of a serious market loss.

But if I was spread out in 50 stocks when the market turned south, selling one or two would give me no protection whatsoever. I'd still be virtually fully invested and would suffer the full effect of the market's overall decline. Remember: when the market goes down, three of four stocks go down with it. Our comprehensive historical studies, which now cover up to 75 years, also show that many stocks, once they've been through a severe decline, don't come back. An investor with a widely diversified portfolio could therefore end up with many stocks that may have been leaders in the past but are now old, unwanted merchandise. These holdings can languish for years, diluting the overall percentage results an investor can achieve.

You can also diversify more wisely by taking your stock positions in a more deliberate, measured way. Never, ever commit all your funds in one decision. Instead, commit them little by little over time—and then only after the other holdings in your portfolio are beginning to show progress. In this way, you are diversifying in time, and only if things are going your way. If they aren't, why keep putting in more money? You should never get fully invested until you are making a profit and showing some headway with what you own.

Say you have $100,000 and you've decided to put an equal amount in no more than five stocks. You don't have to commit the full $20,000 the first time you buy each stock. You might contribute half the amount and then, if that begins to work out, slowly commit additional amounts until you've achieved your full $20,000 position.

If you sell your worst-performing stocks as you go along, some of that money can be directed not only into new positions but also into the better stocks you already own, if they're at sound new buying points. In time, you'll find that even a diversified 10-stock portfolio has been pared to 6, 7, or 8 stocks. Your portfolio will still be diversified, but it will be stronger because you will have shifted funds from the weaker performers into the better selections. I call this the force-feeding method.

The market itself will help you in this process by sorting through your selections and separating the wheat (stocks that go up) from the chaff (those that don't). Just make sure you don't argue with its decisions.

There are several ways to add to long-term positions. If you're a very conservative investor, you might take only half-positions on your first buys and then wait to see if they go up 20 to 25 percent. If they do, and then they build whole new bases that seem to be sound, you can make your second, somewhat lesser, buy when they break out from there.

Less conservative investors should add without delay to their positions after they've made their first buy as soon as the stock has moved up between 2 and 3 percent from the precise initial buy price. Just make sure you commit fewer dollars to the second purchase, so you don't run up your average cost too fast. For example, if you bought at

50, and the stock goes to 51, you might buy more just because it's gone to 51 and given you some initial indication you could be on the right track. But if you bought 100 shares the first time, you might buy 65 the second time, feeding a little bit more money into a position that's possibly right. My second buy is almost always automatic and is done as soon as my first buy is up 2 to 2½ percent. That way I won't ever miss adding to a possible winner. A third buy of 35 shares might be added later if the stock trades at 52. But don't pyramid beyond a 5 percent increase from your correct buy point of 50. In this case, don't chase the stock past 52.50 or you'll run the increased risk of getting caught in the next normal price pullback that will eventually occur.

If your initial $50 buy promptly goes down to $48, leave it alone. The last thing you want to do is buy more because the stock is cheaper. That would mean you're arguing with the market, claiming it doesn't know what it's doing. As I've said before, that way lies danger.

There will always be instances where a stock will go from 50 to 51, then roll over and collapse later. But in the long run, you're better off adding to positions in stocks that go up, leaving you with a little more money in those you could be right on and a little less in those you could be wrong on. Always follow up what's working and cut what's not. Pyramid only in bull markets, however. Pyramiding just doesn't work well at all in a bear market, where almost every breakout or rally fails.

In bear markets you should be mainly in cash. For the entire period of the market top in March 2000 through 2002, our internal money management group operating from our holding company had an average of only 10 percent invested in stocks. The rest, due to the negative general market indexes that prevailed, was in money market funds. The few times we tried to reenter the market in a small way, we made no progress and had to retreat by cutting mistakes quickly and going back to money market funds. It was not until March 2003—almost exactly 3 years from the time we moved to cash in 2000—that we returned to a more fully invested position.

You can sell short during a bear market if you are highly experienced and really know what you're doing. When you sell short you'll have to make sure that you can borrow from your broker the stock that you intend to sell. You sell short expecting the stock to go down in price so you can buy it back at a lower price to close out your speculation. But selling short can be risky, and most newcomers who try it lose money.

You never want to sell short a stock that's running up and looks too high to you in price or PE. It could be high for a good reason and could move higher. You also don't want to short thinly traded small-capitalization stocks. It's too easy for someone to run the stock's price up and cause you to lose money and have to cover (buy back) your short position. Finally, you may not want to sell short big dividend-paying stocks because you will have to pay for each dividend that comes due.

Ironically, the best time to short a former market-leading stock is five to seven months after it has clearly broken down and topped and has rallied back three or four times in a sideways basing area and then starts to weaken.

Short selling must be executed in a very precise manner, knowing exactly what you're doing. It's tricky and more difficult to do than buying a stock because there are more wrong times to sell short and only a few really right times when you can more safely risk going short. You shouldn't sell short at a time when it's obvious to most people. The right time is seldom ever when a stock is breaking below an old low that every amateur chartist can see. It's always best to wait until a former huge market leader has very definitely made a major top and is down a number of months from its top.

There should be no question that the stock has topped. Then it's solely a question of precision timing that lets you get short after the third or fourth rally back has forced the premature short sellers to cover their short positions by buying back the stock.

When you go short, you can't afford to wait for a new low price, but must short after the third or fourth rally up to 10 or 20 percent or more starts to fail, the stock falls back below its 10-week moving average price line, and the volume for the day picks up. The stock should always be at least 4 or 5 points above a previous low price a number of weeks ago that some chart followers might view as a new breakdown point or possible support area. This will give you a crucial potential cushion or edge before the stock becomes obvious to most other traders.

It's far too late to short when a stock breaks below a prior low support area. Few investors understand this, and that's why most lose money selling short. Since short selling is more complex, I wouldn't pyramid on the down side more than once, if even that, because it's too easy for the stock to turn on you if the market rallies for several days. Also, you should take your profits when a stock drops 20 to 30 percent while it's still declining, because at some point it will turn and rally rapidly 20 to 50 percent or so, to run in short sellers. After the rapid rally above the stock's 10-week moving average line, the stock can probably be shorted again once it breaks below its 10-week line and volume picks up.

Following are several examples of correct short sale points and the wrong times to attempt short selling. Gil Morales, one of our successful short sellers, provided a few of the examples.

Another consideration in commonsense portfolio management is how much you should commit to stocks in a particular industry group or sector. How many, for example, are in the computer industry, how many in health care, how many in retailing? You don't want excessive exposure to any one group, because you will get hurt if that group suddenly falls out of favor or corrects. If you were loaded up with Internet or technology stocks when the tech bubble burst, you know

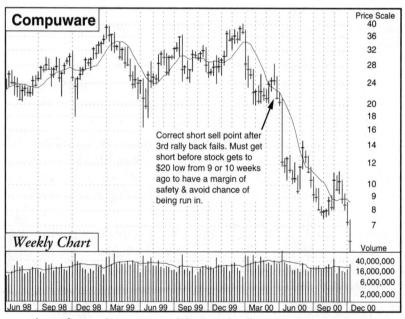

Short After Stock Has Big Breakdown and Rally over 10-Week Line Fails

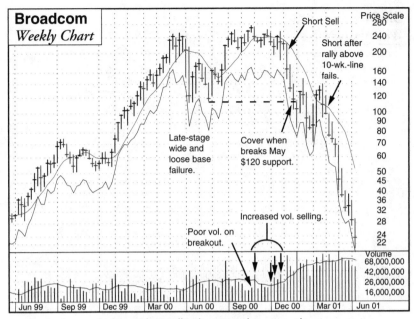

Volume Clues Tell When Broadcom Is a Short

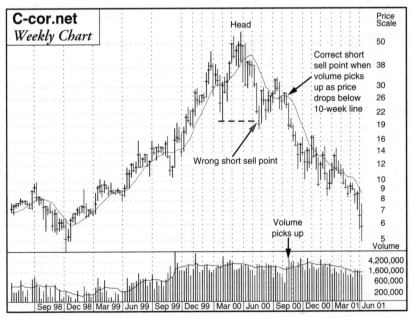

Bad Break to $19 Puts Right Shoulder Below Left Shoulder

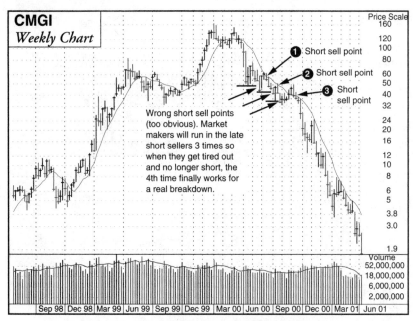

CMGI
Weekly Chart

Price Scale
160
120
100
80

❶ Short sell point
❷ Short sell point
❸ Short sell point

60
50
40
32
24
20
16
12
10
8
6
5
3.8
3.0
1.9

Wrong short sell points (too obvious). Market makers will run in the late short sellers 3 times so when they get tired out and no longer short, the 4th time finally works for a real breakdown.

Volume
52,000,000
18,000,000
6,000,000
2,000,000

Sep 98 | Dec 98 | Mar 99 | Jun 99 | Sep 99 | Dec 99 | Mar 00 | Jun 00 | Sep 00 | Dec 00 | Mar 01 | Jun 01

Safest Short Point Is Nine Months After CMGI's Top

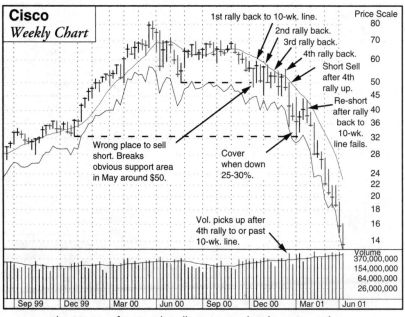

Cisco
Weekly Chart

Price Scale
80

1st rally back to 10-wk. line.
2nd rally back.
3rd rally back.
4th rally back.
Short Sell after 4th rally up.
Re-short after rally back to 10-wk. line fails.

70
60
50
45
40
36
32
28

Wrong place to sell short. Breaks obvious support area in May around $50.

Cover when down 25-30%.

24
22
20
18
16

Vol. picks up after 4th rally to or past 10-wk. line.

14

Volume
370,000,000
154,000,000
64,000,000
26,000,000

Sep 99 | Dec 99 | Mar 00 | Jun 00 | Sep 00 | Dec 00 | Mar 01 | Jun 01

Short Cisco After Fourth Rally Drops Back Below 10-Week Line

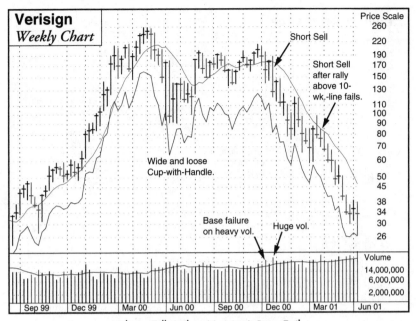

Verisign
Weekly Chart

Price Scale
260
220
190
170
150
130
110
100
90
80
70
60
50
45
38
34
30
26

Short Sell

Short Sell
after rally
above 10-
wk,-line fails.

Wide and loose
Cup-with-Handle.

Base failure
on heavy vol.

Huge vol.

Volume
14,000,000
6,000,000
2,000,000

Sep 99 | Dec 99 | Mar 00 | Jun 00 | Sep 00 | Dec 00 | Mar 01 | Jun 01

Volume Tells When Verisign's Base Fails

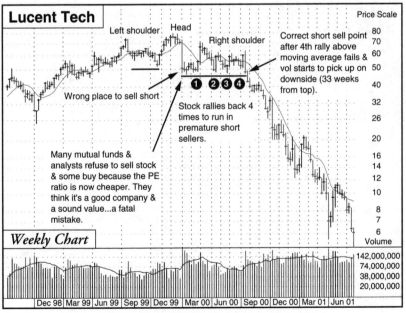

Lucent Tech

Price Scale

Left shoulder   Head

Right shoulder

Correct short sell point
after 4th rally above
moving average fails &
vol starts to pick up on
downside (33 weeks
from top).

80
70
60
50
40
32
26
20
16
14
12
10
8
7
6

Wrong place to sell short

❶ ❷❸❹

Stock rallies back 4
times to run in
premature short
sellers.

Many mutual funds &
analysts refuse to sell stock
& some buy because the PE
ratio is now cheaper. They
think it's a good company &
a sound value...a fatal
mistake.

Weekly Chart

Volume

Dec 98 | Mar 99 | Jun 99 | Sep 99 | Dec 99 | Mar 00 | Jun 00 | Sep 00 | Dec 00 | Mar 01 | Jun 01

142,000,000
74,000,000
38,000,000
20,000,000

Right Shoulder Needs to Drop Below Left Shoulder

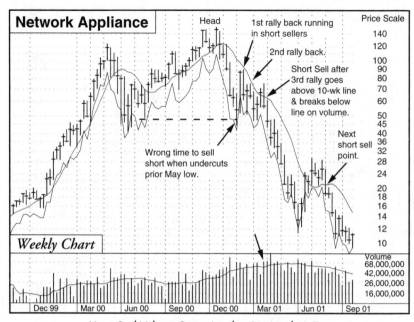

Huge Red Volume Spots Another Big Leader's Top

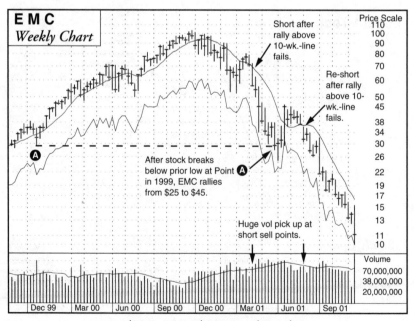

Another Great Leader Tops and Is a Short

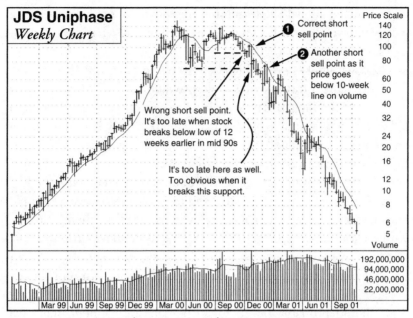

JDS Uniphase
Weekly Chart

Price Scale

① Correct short sell point

② Another short sell point as it price goes below 10-week line on volume

Wrong short sell point. It's too late when stock breaks below low of 12 weeks earlier in mid 90s

It's too late here as well. Too obvious when it breaks this support.

Volume

Mar 99 | Jun 99 | Sep 99 | Dec 99 | Mar 00 | Jun 00 | Sep 00 | Dec 00 | Mar 01 | Jun 01 | Sep 01

Don't Short Too Soon When Everyone Sees It

Yahoo!
Weekly Chart

Price Scale

Correct short sell point (35 weeks from top).

Premature, wrong short sell point. It's too obvious, everyone sees it so they get run in. The exact short sell point is after 4 upward pullbacks in price above the 10-week line. When rally starts to fail & volume picks up on a daily chart for the first time on a down day. You must get short in low $120s to establish a cushion before it gets to prior $110 low.

Volume

Mar 99 | Jun 99 | Sep 99 | Dec 99 | Mar 00 | Jun 00 | Sep 00 | Dec 00 | Mar 01 | Jun 01 | Sep 01

Short When Stock Has Clearly Broken Down and Rallied Back Several Times

107

what I mean. As with determining how many individual stocks you will own in your portfolio, you should set limits on what you'll commit to a single industry category.

My own limit is pretty high—50 to 60 percent. But I've invested for many years. Most people should probably set lower limits. I know what you're thinking: this goes against the concept of concentration we talked about a minute ago, which is a key to making big money when you're right. And indeed it does. But here again, you can make exceptions if you are experienced, know what you're doing, and are willing to always execute your strict selling disciplines to protect yourself.

If you own the very best stocks in the very best industry group—and if you're ahead a fair amount in those stocks—there's nothing wrong with ending up with 50 or 60 percent of your portfolio in one sector. As we saw in the tech boom, however, most people can't handle that much group concentration. You have to be fast on your feet because you have substantially more risk exposure. So, a more typical limit should probably be 25 to 30 percent. Remember, high-tech stocks are 2 to 2½ times as volatile as most other stock categories. You can get hurt badly if you're concentrated in them, or worse, own them on margin or have used borrowed money.

One principle mentioned earlier is: don't ever average down on any stock in your portfolio. If you buy a stock at $50 and it goes to $45, never buy more. Yes, sometimes you'll get away with it—but no more often than you will drawing an inside straight in poker. In the long run, mathematics will work against you, and sooner or later you will get hurt badly.

Be wary of any broker who advises you to buy more of a stock that's down from your initial purchase price; in essence, he or she is telling you to throw good money after bad. Find another, smarter broker. Here again, human nature is coming into play. It's easier for someone to tell you that a stock he or she recommended or you decided to buy is an even better buy now that it's cheaper than it is to admit he or she was wrong, that a possible mistake has been made, and that you've got to sell to cut your loss. Even brokers who know this will have a hard time saying it because it's the last thing their customers want to hear. Astute professionals average up, not down.

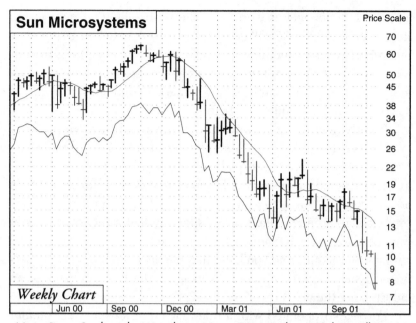

Sun Microsystems

Price Scale

Weekly Chart

| Jun 00 | Sep 00 | Dec 00 | Mar 01 | Jun 01 | Sep 01 |

Never Buy a Stock on the Way down, Never Average down, and Cut All Losses Quickly . . . Otherwise This Could Happen to You—Sun Microsystems Reached $2.34 in 2002, down 96 Percent

Don't confuse averaging down, however, with adding to stocks on pullbacks after they've gone up a bit. You may be presented with a buy point, for example, if a stock you bought out of a proper base at 50 rose to, say, 57, then pulled back to 53 or 54 and bounced off its 10-week moving average line with a strong pickup in volume. This is not averaging down (your first buy was at 50); this is averaging up. Just remember: never put more money into something unless the first amount is working. Generally, you can get away with adding to an outstanding market leader after it's out of its base on its first two price pullbacks to its 10-week moving average price line.

Another sound principle for quality professional portfolio management is to avoid cheap stocks that sell for very low prices or are very thinly traded (low average daily trading volume). Again, there are always exceptions, but as a general rule, everything sells for about what it's worth at the time. A $20 stock is worth $20, a $10 stock is worth $10, a $5 stock is worth $5. The probability that most cheap stock selling at $2 or $5 will go up a lot is reasonably low. It's down at that price because something's wrong with it in the first place. By contrast, the $50, $75, or $100 stock sells at that price because it's been more successful. And in the right bull market conditions, the odds of its going higher are quite a bit better.

If nothing else, big institutions can't take million-share positions in $2 stocks. They have large sums of money to employ, and they don't like to get involved in lower-quality stocks that have poor marketability or lower-grade sponsorship. If you own a $2 or $5 stock, to whom do you sell it when something goes wrong? There just aren't many professionals around willing to buy stocks in that category. What you want behind your companies is big, informed professional buying and strong sponsorship. And you'll get that mainly in high-quality, higher-priced issues. You're supposed to look for the best company in an industry, not the worst.

For years I operated with a rule that I'd never buy stocks under $20 a share. At times I've lowered that to $15 for a few NASDAQ stocks. But I've always tried to avoid what's considered the low-quality, cheap stocks category, viewing that as more or less the junk pile. This is the reason *Investor's Business Daily* lists stocks priced under $10 separately, so they don't clutter tables of higher-priced, higher-quality issues. It also saves you valuable time when you're checking out the more important main stock tables.

It's human nature to think that if you deal in low-priced stocks you can buy more shares and make a lot of money fast. Most amateur or novice investors think this way. But it simply isn't true. What you're really dealing in are significantly more speculative stocks with less-proven records and less institutional sponsorship. So the probability of major lasting success is less and the risk of greater loss is increased. I've seen many otherwise intelligent people who were never able to recognize or break this bad gambler's habit.

Don't think in terms of how many shares you can buy, but in terms of, "I have so many dollars to invest, and I'm going to put those dollars in the very best investments I can find." The very best investments usually don't sell at $5 and $10 a share. And if you don't buy $5 stocks, you certainly want to avoid penny stocks. They're even worse—much worse.

Some people feel embarrassed to call their broker with an order to buy anything less than a round lot, or 100 shares, of a stock. These people need to get over it. They're far better off buying an odd lot (fewer than 100 shares) of a quality company than 100 or 500 shares of a low-priced issue. Invest your hard-earned dollars in the best stocks you can find, in whatever number of shares you can afford. If that comes out to only 5, 10, or 20 shares, so be it.

The median price of the 50 top-performing stocks from 1997 to 2000 when they broke out of their initial bases in that period was $46.78, and these stocks' median price advance was 1031% over 61 weeks' time. PE ratios at the beginning breakout points of the best-performing stocks from 1960 to 1995 had a median of 36 times current earnings before their huge price moves and PE expansion of more than 100 percent.

You also don't need a lot of money to get started in the market. I began with $500. Over time, you can add to your holdings as you save money. And as you learn to invest better by reading and studying, your money will in time grow. I'd also advise against trying to get rich quick by excessive trading in options or futures. These instruments are highly leveraged, and overemphasis or overtrading in these areas entails substantially greater risk of loss.

Another important concept—like diversification—that's widely promoted and certainly makes prudent sense on the surface, but in its real-world execution is not always the optimum profit-making way to manage a portfolio, is what is known as asset allocation. Yes, everyone needs to figure out how much money they need to live on, how much they need for emergencies, how much they need to save, and how much they're going to invest. And then, out of that investment nest egg, they need to figure how much will go into common stocks.

But many investors, at the urging of their advisors, go much further. They'll determine what percentages will be allocated not only to common stocks, but to preferred stocks, to bonds, to foreign equities, to gold, and so forth and so on. Here again, the aim is wide diversification: the more categories you are invested in, the safer you'll be. If you are very, very conservative, this is of value. But allocating assets in this way guarantees only one thing: a more mediocre overall result. If you use proven sell rules to reduce portfolio risk when appropriate, I see little reason to have a meaningful allocation in corporate bonds or bond funds.

Asset allocation is sound as long as it is limited mainly to common stocks and cash or money market equivalents. In other words, the allocation is kept simple. Protection in a bad market comes from selling common stocks and moving back into cash or money market instruments. It does not come from, say, moving from 55 percent stocks to 50 percent and increasing your bond position by 5 or 10 percent. Investors who allocate assets might also raise or lower their allocations too late or at the wrong time. Besides, allocation is not a guarantee against losing in a bear market: if you're 70 percent in stocks, and you cut your allocation to 60 percent, and you're in a terrible bear market, you still could lose heavily, because the change is too small to make a significant difference. Other investors could lower their equity allocation late in the game and move more into bonds and then fail to move back into stocks in a timely manner once the market has definitely hit bottom and begun a major new uptrend. An allocator must therefore make two decisions correctly: when to pull back and when to reenter.

Moreover, some investments can dramatically underperform even in a bull market. Foreign stocks fall into this category. So does gold, which will go nowhere for many booming market years and then make a strong, short-lived bear market move that's then held up as justification for its perpetual longer-term ownership.

Like diversification, excessive asset allocation is a hedge against ignorance—in this case, ignorance of how to invest more soundly. But it gives some advisors a widely accepted, prudent reason to go back to their clients during the year to make adjustments in their accounts in the hope of improving or protecting results. Whether the asset shifts they recommend always pay off for most investors depends on the realistic experience of the advisor or the analysts employed by the advisor's investment firm. Investigations in 2002 inferred that the records of some Wall Street strategists who recommend the allocations might leave something to be desired.

Make no mistake, though: managing a more concentrated portfolio of common stocks takes discipline and skill. Keeping your profit-to-loss ratio at 3 to 1 by cutting losses at 7 to 8 percent and frequently even less, taking some of your profits at 20 to 25 percent, and holding your few real winners longer requires you to stay on your toes. There will be occasional times, though, when a loss will get away from you, and a stock suddenly drops 15 or 20 percent from your cost. When this happens, it's even more urgent that you sell that stock. Abrupt, excessive breaks that lead to an abnormal loss can be signaling that a company might be getting into really serious trouble.

I mention this because many people, once this happens to them, become psychologically frozen. They decide they'll wait for the stock to rally back so they can sell it at where they should have sold it in the first place. Or they'll think it's down so much it can't go any lower, or that the loss happened so fast or is so large they just don't want to take it. Whatever the case, they're not coming to grips with the realistic fact that the more a stock goes down, the more reason there is to correct the situation before it does even more serious damage. A tiny campfire not extinguished can develop into a devastating forest fire.

One other point: when you decide to buy or sell a stock, do it at the market—that is, at whatever price the stock is selling for at the time. If you use limit orders, insisting that the stock be sold or bought at a specific price, the day will come when you'll miss your limit price and you won't get out of something you want out of or into something you want to own. You're not investing to squeeze another quarter-point out of a stock. You're investing for a much bigger potential than that.

Sometimes, what you don't do while managing a portfolio is as important as what you do. Following are a few examples.

Price-to-earnings ratios, dividends, and book values. In bull markets, at least, I wouldn't pay so much attention to these oft-cited measures at all. Most of what you need to know about PEs is that the best companies generally sell at higher ratios and the others at lower ones. (Do the best basketball, football, or baseball stars come at the lowest prices or salaries?) The very best-performing companies for the past 50 years have been those that are growing steadily and paying little or no dividends because the money they earn is reinvested in R&D, new products, or expansion. If a young or midsize company is still growing and pays out cash in dividends, the company will have to make up for it later by borrowing, and that costs the shareholders interest expense.

Most economists who are enamored with dividend theory never seem to understand this.

Dividends can only be paid out of earnings, and it's earnings you must always evaluate. Stocks go up in price because of improving growth in earnings per share, not dividend yield. In all my years of dealing with over 600 major mutual fund money managers, I've never had any ask me about a company's dividend. It's always about expected sales and earnings growth and the quality of the company's management and new products. In fact, the smartest money managers know that when a company finally starts paying a dividend or increases its dividend payout ratio, it's usually been a tip-off that the company is no longer growing.

If you need income, you might consider buying the very best proven, consistent quality companies and withdrawing 6 percent a year from your overall account rather than buying more lackluster, older, maintainer, dividend-paying companies solely to provide income. If you do buy dividend stocks, don't buy those with the absolute highest yields. They usually are lower in quality, involve greater risk, and could therefore perform more poorly. The new lower federal tax rates on dividends will be an added benefit to most older retired dividend-seeking investors.

As for book value, you'd be hard pressed to find a strong link between this accounting measure and stock performance.

Closed-end funds. Some investors whose portfolios include mutual funds will have closed-end funds promoted to them. These should generally be avoided. Closed-end funds are not like open-end mutual funds, which are obligated to buy back shares at whatever their current asset value happens to be. Closed-end funds are traded like stocks in an auction market and can go to any price. In other words, if the asset value of a company is $15, there's nothing to prevent the stock from going to $7 to $8 and selling at a 50 percent discount for years.

Bonds. I would also not buy bonds, especially as a "safe haven" when the stock market is selling off. You're just as well off in money market funds or government securities that are absolutely safe. You can lose money in bonds just as you can in stocks. Fortunes were lost in bonds during the Depression. And bonds do not provide a worthwhile return over time; in many cases, they haven't even kept up with inflation and taxes. You also may be paying a commission to buy bond funds.

Balanced and industry funds.　These should also be avoided in most instances. A balanced fund has so much in equities and so much in bonds, which almost guarantees an inferior result. Industry funds will act the same as stocks: they'll go up faster when an industry is doing well and come down faster when it isn't. If you buy a high-tech fund, for example, you might do well for a short period. But when the tech sector gets into trouble, you can suffer serious losses. An industry fund simply doesn't provide the same degree of longer-term protection you get with an equity mutual fund diversified across a broad cross section of industries or an index mutual fund.

Foreign stocks.　I'm no fan of these either. Thousands of solid, home-grown companies trade on the U.S. markets. If you can't find a decent one here, you're not going to find it in France, Germany, Hong Kong, or Brazil. Besides, what do you know about those countries' currencies or government policy? For example, do they encourage the formation and growth of new entrepreneurial companies? And how are you going to keep close track of foreign markets?

Most of this runs counter to what you hear from much-quoted "experts." But you must realize that when it comes to the stock market, consensus thinking and conventional wisdom can be deadly. The vast majority of investors don't do well because they haven't done enough detailed homework to really discover or understand realistic investment principles.

When you go to a doctor, you can assume you're dealing with a professional who is truly a highly trained specialist in his or her field and who uses proven methods. In the securities sales field, you are usually dealing with smart, educated, very fluent people. But, unlike doctors, some may not have years of professional, successful stock market experience or realistic analytical or portfolio training. In addition, the stock market itself is far more complicated than most people realize. So it's not so easy to find an outstanding professional who can give sound advice on a consistent basis over a period of time. To get to that point takes a great deal of objective hard work, study, and discipline.

There are many in the industry who are dedicated, capable, and qualified. But you must do your due diligence—insisting on successful references or referrals and asking lots of questions about their investment beliefs, methods, policies, and sources of ideas and analysis in addition to their firm's research. You also definitely need to learn and know enough about the field of investments to recognize sound, competent advice when you hear it. Most investors give this process of whom they deal with, consult with, or listen to less time and thought than they do buying a washing machine or a car.

It should help you if you know for certain your broker has attended one or more of IBD's paid workshops. In these all-day sessions, we train people on how to read charts and follow sound fundamental buy and sell rules. It also could be a plus if your broker has read and reread at least one of our three books on the market. Also, find out if your broker is motivated enough to subscribe to IBD on his or her own, or just looks at the office copy from time to time. You want to see real dedicated skill, knowledge, and extra effort being put forth.

Finally, a few words on commissions and taxes. Commissions charged by brokers to buy and sell shares in the "very best" companies can be viewed in much the same way. The 0.5 to 2 percent commissions charged on stock transactions are actually relatively minor compared with what you pay to buy most other things. That shirt you bought at a department store was probably marked up 33 percent. Food at a grocery store has a 25 percent markup, and furniture and jewelry can carry markups as high as 50 percent. When you buy and sell real estate, someone gets a 6 percent commission going in and a 6 percent commission coming out. Compared with the alternatives, in other words, commonsense investing in common stocks is not only a privilege and an opportunity, it can be a relative bargain.

The superior liquidity of stocks is not always present in business, art, or other investments. Liquid markets provide tremendous safety for you once you learn how and when you should sell stocks as well as buy them.

Taxes also seem to give a lot of investors pause. Many say they won't sell a stock because they don't want to pay the taxes on the gain. Usually, if they stay with the stock too long, their worries will be over: they won't have to pay a tax because they will no longer have a gain. Always make your buy or sell decisions based first on the stock. Tax considerations should be a distant second.

Uncle Sam's participation in your profits is part of the price of being highly successful in your investing. It's better to pay whatever taxes you owe than to lose money and not have to pay at all or to get a tax shelter that winds up losing money as an investment or being questioned by the government.

If it helps, look at taxpaying as a privilege of having the opportunity to share in the success of hundreds of outstanding entrepreneurial companies. Many other countries don't give their citizens that opportunity. Nor do they encourage entrepreneurs to go out and start new companies. As a result, entrepreneurs have a hard time obtaining financing, so there are not that many great companies to invest in in the first place.

America is full of outstanding opportunities, and once you learn how to recognize and take advantage of them, you will always have to pay your fair share of taxes. But that's a small price to pay for the chance to make a better life for yourself and your loved ones.

A few further observations follow.

When it comes to making money in the stock market, the best brains aren't always those based in New York City and backed by armies of analysts. They are more likely to be found among the top portfolio managers headquartered in 10 to 15 other major cities throughout the U.S. In fact, you are just as likely to find top-performing portfolio managers with addresses in Boston, Dallas, and Los Angeles as you are on Wall Street. One place you normally won't find them, however, is on the nation's college campuses, especially in economics departments. University economics professors are exceptionally bright, intelligent, valuable people, but many have little realistic understanding of the stock market and even less highly profitable experience in it. Many have never run a successful business. Instead, they may frequently tend to cling to theories and academic beliefs that haven't necessarily worked out so well in the realistic but contrary battlefield of our auction marketplace.

The random walk and efficient market theories that some university professors have promoted have proved mainly to be ivory tower academic nonsense. So have most dividend discount models and formula plan investing, which years ago led Yale University to sell and move heavily to cash at the start of a booming new bull market. There are, however, some finance and investment professors who have become serious, down-to-earth students of the market and teach some of the real-world methods we've been discussing.

Honesty, ethics, and humility are much more important qualifications for the successful investor than a big ego or high IQ. You must always be willing to analyze, discuss, and admit your many mistakes in the market. That's really how we all learn and get smarter. It may also be why women do just as well as or sometimes better than men when it comes to investing. They seem to be less stubborn and ego oriented in hanging onto old market myths and more receptive to reading and learning sounder investing methods.

After many years, I've concluded that successful stock selection is 60 to 65 percent knowing every key fundamental fact about a company and its industry and 35 to 40 percent understanding chart and market action. All my best winners over the years have had big increases in earnings and sales as well as strong profit margins and a high return on equity. They were at the time the top companies in their industries in those basic measurements, and virtually all sold for higher-than-normal PE ratios. I may have been initially drawn to many of them by their chart or market action, but they would never have worked so well if they hadn't possessed the necessary powerful fundamentals, institutional sponsorship, and revolutionary new products or services.

It'll always be the extra work and effort you put into any endeavor that pays off. It's all the little important details you learn by repeated study and observation that add to your knowledge and skill and make the difference between succeeding and almost making it in the investment world.

Following are a few final charts of outstanding past companies I've selected at random that show you what enormous potential has always been there in America's stock market once you learn how to invest with realistic portfolio management rules and principles.

Syntex was my first really big winner, bought in July 1963 and sold six months later. I didn't know anyone else who bought it then because it looked too high to everyone. It scared people because it had already doubled in price, it was selling for a new high of $100 a share (the chart is adjusted for a 3-for-1 split), its PE ratio was 45, and the company had some lawsuits filed against it that claimed its product caused breast cancer. But the sales and earnings were growing rapidly and the product was truly revolutionary—the pill, which was to change all of society.

Sea Containers had a perfect cup-with-a-handle pattern. Notice the extreme volume dry-ups in the handle as the price pulled back and had many tight closing weeks. Remember, the only good stocks are the ones that go up, so if you miss the first proper buy point, be patient and in time the stock will form another base and give you a new buy point if it is truly a good stock. One tip-off that Sea Containers was good is that the price advanced 50 percent on a big acceleration in trading volume in its first four weeks.

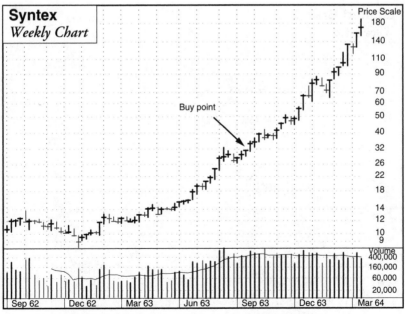

High Is Not Always High . . . Sometimes It's Low

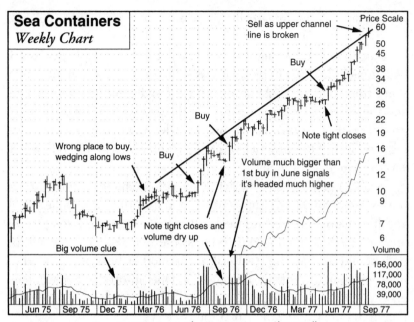

Sea Containers, a Classic Big Cup-with-Handle

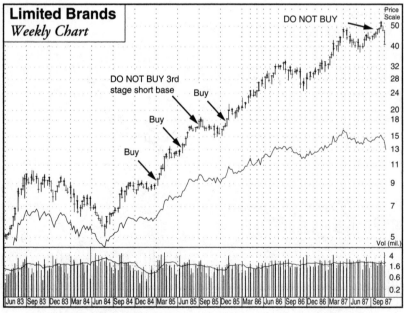

Limited Is a Big 79-Week Cup-with-Handle, Up 420 Percent in 113 Weeks

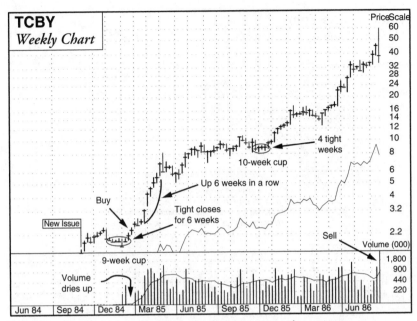

TCBY's 1984 Nine-Week Cup Goes up More Than 20 Times

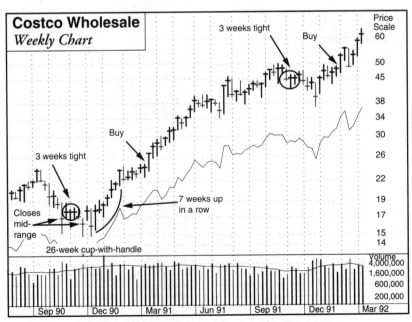

Costco Is a Follow-on to Price Co.'s Earlier Huge Move

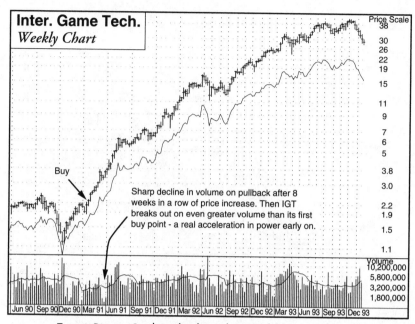

Twenty Percent Stock Buyback Leads to 15-fold Price Advance

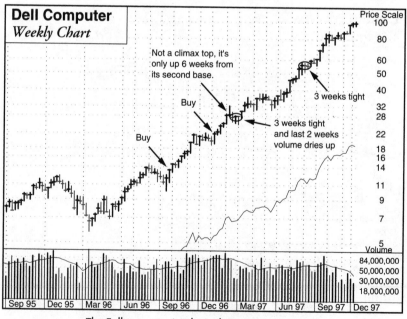

The Follow-on to Apple and Compaq Computer

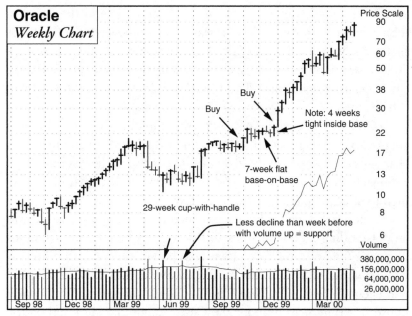

Cup-with-Handle Followed by a Flat Base-on-Base

Price Co. Double Bottom-with-Handle Saw a 1293 Percent Increase

123

The Limited women's retail stores benefited from the trend of more women in the workplace. It was an awesome leader of the 1980s that just kept going, building a series of bases until it built a late-stage faulty base in 1987. (Again, all chart presentations are adjusted for any stock splits, so don't think The Limited's initial buy was at $9; it was actually $27.)

TCBY was an exciting new issue that rapidly expanded its frozen yogurt stores to capitalize on the yogurt fad in 1984. Even buying it a year later coming out of its 10-week cup pattern in the last quarter of 1985 yielded a remarkable profit, again proving that what may seem high to most people may actually be low.

Costco is a stock I missed, for which there was no excuse. It was an outstanding follow-on stock to Price Co., which I had owned for 3½ years. One of the Costco founders, James Sinegal, had originally worked with Sol Price, who started the warehouse store concept in San Diego. A few years later, Sinegal opened the same style of warehouse stores in Seattle under the Costco name. Be alert and on the lookout for solid future follow-on opportunities to market leaders of the last few years.

Here's another compelling example of follow-on stocks. First, Apple Computer was the leader years ago, then Compaq Computer; then Dell assumed leadership with its new concept of direct sales of PCs made to order.

International Game Technology gave an unmistakable clue when it announced a 10 percent buyback of its stock and then a few months later a bold second 10 percent buyback. Its new computerized gaming machines produced an incredible 15-fold price advance for its stock.

Oracle had already proven itself as a leader in database software before its classic base on base formed. Notice the four weeks of tight closes on its second base just before it exploded to the upside.

Price Co., owner of the Price Club Warehouse discount stores, was another one of my best winners, first purchased in the second quarter of 1982, when it only had two stores. It performed in excellent fashion for 3½ years, until the company expanded to the East Coast and the management became a little stretched. Price Co. was the original leader and innovator in a new concept of merchandising carried on later by Costco. Price Co.'s return on equity was an impos-ing 55 percent.

When you're right on your selection and timing, you should see your stock move up shortly after your initial buy, providing you a little cushion. A good cushion allows you the margin to make a few smaller follow-up buys after your initial purchase. It will also help you survive if some publication tries to attack and derail your stock because they think the stock's PE is too high. In most cases, that's like saying Michael Jordan wasn't worth what he was paid when in his prime with the Chicago Bulls. When this happens to an outstanding company with solid earnings and sales growth, I've found the resulting panic selling usually only lasts from two hours to as much as two days and in many cases may create a sound buying opportunity for knowledgeable professionals.

History is filled with examples of conventional wisdom, unsound personal opinions, and naysayers who turned out to be all wet. Lord Duveen made a fortune years ago by paying what seemed to most people to be overly high prices for one-of-a-kind paintings by the old masters in Europe and selling them for substantially higher prices to America's then-new entrepreneurs, such as Henry Ford. Critics all thought CNN's Ted Turner paid too much for MGM's film library, which he ultimately capitalized on over and over again.

British inventors said Thomas Edison couldn't create a light bulb with the methods he was using. The Wright brothers were crazy to think they could fly like birds. Billy Mitchell was wrong about the potential future of air power. The Navy thought a gravel contractor named Henry Kaiser couldn't possibly know how to build ships. Alexander Graham Bell offered the president of Western Union part ownership in his new invention, the telephone, and was turned down with the question, "What could I do with an interesting toy like that?" William Henry Seward's folly was paying the Russians $7 million for an overpriced piece of worthless snow and ice now known as Alaska.

To be a successful investor, you need to do your homework and evaluate as many relevant facts as you can get your hands on. That way you'll have more confidence in your own ability, and then you'll stop being influenced or adversely affected by other people's opinions, no matter how strongly or widely they may be held or how authoritative you assume the source or medium to be.

For serious investors, Daily Graphs Online has a premium service offering sophisticated daily and weekly charts, data screening on over 100 data items, and industry group analysis. For a trial, visit www. dailygraphs.com.

I believe in history and facts rather than listening to personal opinions. So here's the realistic history of the stocks that have led each bull market and economic recovery in recent years—the period of America's greatest growth rate and unparalleled economic and social progress. It amounts to a kaleidoscopic summary of how our nation really grows.

This amazing growth story is told and retold cycle after cycle because the American system is based on freedom and opportunity for everyone who has the desire and motivation to do the work and study necessary to become successful. Each economic cycle is led by companies that create outstanding new products, new time- and money-saving inventions, new technologies, and new needed services. This unparalleled growth will continue—but only as long as our freedoms are protected and defended. The government needs to keep out of the way by cutting excessive taxes and wasteful spending. Then innovators, inventors, and entrepreneurs will have the incentive to keep on improving everyone's standard of living and opportunities.

Note in the table how most companies that lead in one cycle do not lead in the next. Note also how each cycle's leaders had new products and that high earnings growth or EPS Ratings were behind all the real successes. Recent IPOs were a powerful factor in the country's growth, particularly since 1970, and dividends were not.

To make these things happen, a strong, sustainable economy and stock market are absolutely key. That's why I sent the following letter to President Bush on July 6, 2002, when our economy and market were struggling. Earlier in February I had tried unsuccessfully to get a similar letter to the president through Glenn Hubbard, after Dr. Hubbard, head of the president's economic council, spoke at IBD's 2002 Economic Conference in LA. The July 6 letter was also likely sidelined to the president's economic group, since he didn't see it until October, when Katie Boyd, a San Francisco friend

75% of Market Leaders in Each Cycle Were New Companies Incorporated in Prior Ten Years, 80% Paid No Dividends, Earning Growth Was the Driver of Market Leaders, Not Dividends

Company name	Company description	Percent increase	Years of move	Date inc	Date IPO	EPS*	Div.
		1982–1986					
Adobe Systems	New printing software	482	6 months	1983	1986	66	none
Circuit City	New discount electronics store	1971	4¼ years	1949	1986	298%	0.7%
Compaq Computers	New faster, smaller, portable computers	378	11 months	1982	1983	98	none
Costco	New wholesale membership stores	700	3¼ years	1983	1985	92	none
Duquesne Systems	New IBM software	725	2 years	1970	1984	88	none
Emulex	New disk/tape controllers	410	8 months	1979	1981	66%	none
Ford	New management turnaround	173	1 year	1919		158%	none
Franklin Research	New mutual fund company	750	1¼ years	1969	1983	92	1.0%
Genentech	First biotech drug company	277	6 months	1976	1979	82	none
Gillette	Premium-quality world brands	279	3¾ years	1917		72	1.4%
Home Depot	New discount building supply centers	938	1¼ years	1978	1981	140%	none
King World	Syndication new game shows— Wheel of Fortune and Jeopardy	300	1 year	1984	1984	89	none
Laidlaw Transportation	School buses	567	2¾ years	1979	1983	75	none
Limited Stores	Clothing for women in the workplace	467	2¾ years	1963	1973	79	0.9%
Liz Claiborne	Clothing for women in the workplace	2820%	4¾ years	1976	1981	33%	none

(Continued)

75% of Market Leaders in Each Cycle Were New Companies Incorporated in Prior Ten Years, 80% Paid No Dividends, Earning Growth Was the Driver of Market Leaders, Not Dividends (Continued)

Company name	Company description	Percent increase	Years of move	Date inc	Date IPO	EPS*	Div.
Marion Labs	New drugs.	176	10 months	1952		7%	2.0%
Merck	Prescription drugs	270	1¾ years	1934		79	2.8%
Novell	New LAN software	100	5 months	1983	1985	99	none
Price Co.	New wholesale membership stores	1293	4 years	1976	1980	43%	none
Reebok	Tennis, aerobic, and running shoes	262	4 months	1979	1985	97	none
TCBY	Franchise yogurt stores	2290	1½ years	1984	1984	99	none
Wal-Mart	New chain of discount stores	957	3 years	1969	1971	40%	1.1%
1988–1997							
Alliance Semi	Semiconductors for PCs	589	11 months	1985	1993	66	none
America Online	Access to Internet—a new communication medium	647	1½ years	1985	1992	90	none
America Power Conv.	New uninterruptible power supplies for PCs	808	1¾ years	1981	1988	99	none
Amgen	New biotech drugs for cancer patients	680	1¾ years	1980	1983	94	none
Apple South	Applebee's restaurants	463	1¼ years	1986	1991	96	0.1%
Ascend Comm.	New LAN and WAN access products	3206	1¾ years	1989	1994	91	none
Callaway Golf	Big Bertha clubs	333	11 months	1982	1992	99	none
Cisco Systems	New routers and networking equipment	74445	9½ years	1984	1990	99	none

Company	Description						
Cobra Golf	Quality golf clubs	156	6 months	1978	1993	99	none
Dell Computer	New build-to-order PC sales	2973	2½ years	1984	1988	55	none
Digital Switch	New telecommunications switching gear	584	8 months	1976	1980	-106%	none
EMC	New computer storage products	500	1 year	1979	1986	90	none
Int. Game Tech	New microprocessor gaming	1567	2½ years	1980	1981	91	none
Kohl's	New discount department stores	177	1½ years	1988	1982	67	none
Medical Care Int.	Surgical care center	627	3 years	1981	1983	69	none
Mercury Finance	Provides financing for new and used cars	424	2¾ years	1984	1989	98	1.8%
Micron Technology	DRAM and SRAM for computers	300	7 months	1978	1984	99	0.4%
Microsoft	New computer software	13847	10 years	1981	1986	95	none
Newbridge Networks	New worldwide networking products	699	11 months	1986	1989	81	none
Peoplesoft	New HR management software	395	1¼ years	1987	1992	99	none
St. Jude Medical	Leader in prosthetic heart valves	400	2¼ years	1976	1977	85	none
Surgical Care Affiliates	Surgical care center	1636	2¾ years	1982	1983	93	none
Tellabs	Data communication and networking	1074	2¼ years	1974	1980	77	none
Three Com	Computer networking	286	1¼ years	1979	1984	97	none
U S Health Care	New HMOs	125	6 months	1982	1983	90	none

(Continued)

75% of Market Leaders in Each Cycle Were New Companies Incorporated in Prior Ten Years,
80% Paid No Dividends, Earning Growth Was the Driver of Market Leaders, Not Dividends (*Continued*)

Company name	Company description	Percent increase	Years of move	Date inc	Date IPO	EPS*	Div.
United Healthcare	New HMOs	384	1¼ years	1977	1984	91	0.1%
Yahoo!	Access to the Internet	7443	2½ years	1995	1996	52	none
Business Objects	New database software	535	8 months	1990	1994	95	none
1998–2000							
Biogen	New biomedical drugs	330	1½ years	1978	1983	71	none
Charles Schwab	No. 1 online discount broker	439	6 months	1971	1987	91	0.3%
Checkpoint Software	Database software	1142	9 months	1993	1996	97	none
Comverse Technology	New hardware for telephone companies	606	1¼ years	1984	1986	96	none
eBay	New auctions on Internet	1070	6 months	1996	1998	53	none
Etek Dynamics	Fiber-optic equipment	507	6 months	1983	1998	99	none
Network Appliance	New storage devices for networks	517	4 months	1992	1995	98	none
Nokia	Leading cell phone manufacturer	800	2 years	1967	1994	95	none
Oracle Systems	New database software	274	5 months	1977	1986	95	none
PMC-Sierra	New semiconductors	1949	1¼ years	1983	1991	51	none
Qlogic	Integrated circuits for peripheral equipment	3351	1¾ years	1992	1994	68	none

130

Company	Description						
Qualcomm	New cell phone system	2567	1 year	1981	1991	79	none
RF Micro Devices	Integrated circuits for wireless communications	3224	1½ years	1991	1997	68	none
SDL Inc	Fiber-optic equipment	3631	1¼ years	1983	1995	92	none
Siebel Systems	New marketing software	420	7 months	1993	1996	99	none
Sun Microsystems	New leading network products	688	1½ years	1982	1986	94	none
Uniphase	New fiber-optic equipment	2016	1¼ years	1979	1993	90	none
Veritas	New security software	1097	1¼ years	1982	1993	99	none
Vitesse Semi	High-speed chips for Internet devices	535	1¼ years	1987	1991	98	none

*When a percentage is given, it shows an average of prior two quarters' EPS percent increases.
When a number is given, it shows the EPS Rating, a William O'Neil + Co. rating, with 99 being highest.

of his, handed him a copy at a White House dinner. The president replied with a handwritten letter the next day saying that the letter made sense and that he was intrigued with the small business creation idea. I was surprised to receive such a quick reply, since he had plenty on his plate with the war on terrorism plus the pending Iraq problem. But President Bush's administration is proving to be straightforward, businesslike, and responsive on vital economic and international issues.

Since then, there have been a number of changes. Interest rates were finally lowered again, a new Congress has taken over, a new economic team has been installed, the threat of terrorism is being dealt with, 50 million Iraqis and Afghans have been given freedom rather than a brutal dictatorship, and a tax-cutting growth package that will help all taxpayers and our economy has been passed by Congress and signed by the president.

There is a sound reason why more stimulus than normal was definitely needed in 2003. In the aftermath of other serious prolonged stock market periods similar to our 2000 to 2002 bubble, such as 1973 to 1974 and 1929 to 1932, our economy recovered more slowly and needed far more help than normal. And this time we had the psychological damage from 9-11 to contend with.

The deficit is simply not our real problem. During recessions and periodic short wars, deficits are quite normal. And the 2002 deficit as a percentage of our GDP is not out of line. It's only 1.5 percent of the GDP. The average over the last 50 years was 1.9 percent. The amount of net interest we spend servicing the debt that results from those deficits is likewise small, just 1.6 percent of the GDP. The deficit argument, at this point in time, is primarily a political argument used to scare or sway voters to discourage tax reductions.

The way to solve the deficit problem is to invigorate the economy with significant tax cuts and control less critical spending so we will grow our way out of the deficit by increasing government tax receipts. The two major tax cuts since World War II—those enacted during the Kennedy and Reagan administrations—didn't reduce the government's income; they both significantly increased it.

The same thing has happened after every lowering of the tax on capital gains: our government's revenue from capital gains taxes rose.

July 16, 2002

The President
The White House
1600 Pennsylvania Avenue NW
Washington, D.C. 20500

Dear Mr. President:

We met briefly at the photo shoot for Bill Simon in Los Angeles.

Here's a bold new idea that will help you with our sluggish economy and stock market and put you on the offensive with fresh new plans like you've carried out so successfully in the war on terrorism:

Ask Congress ASAP to allow any American who wants to start a new business to pay no income tax on the business for the first two years and only one-half the normal rate the next two years. Also let principals or employees who own stock in the new company pay only one-half the normal capital gains rate on stock they sell in the first 10 years.

This will create a stampede of new entrepreneurial small businesses in America. As you pointed out, they create most of our new jobs. Bigger, older businesses downsize.

It will not cost our government anything since the huge <u>increase</u> in start-ups will be companies that do not now exist. Few new businesses make much in the first year or two. But they will create, on their own initiative, without further government interference or restrictions, several hundred thousand <u>new jobs</u> and <u>new individual taxpayers</u>. That's positive for the economy and high unemployment rate.

With a title like the "Small New Business Creation Act" or the "New Entrepreneurial Business and Jobs Act," Democrats will have a hard time voting against it. It will also eliminate their objection to big business tax cuts, and particularly capital gains cuts, as "only for the rich." This is for all Americans. The common man and woman.

There are crucial reasons to get on the offensive now with positive new economic ideas and to not let opponents and the liberal media try to put you on the defensive.

Eighty percent of stock market winners that drove the 1990s technology boom were companies that had IPOs in their prior eight years and were newly incorporated after the capital gains cut in the 1980s (Dell, Sun Microsystems, Compaq, Amgen, EMC Corp., Oracle, etc.).

History shows new bull markets are usually led by new leaders, not fallen former leaders of the past cycle. We now have few new IPOs to lead a future market recovery.

I'm not sure everyone in Washington understands the real cause of, or answer to, what's happened in the stock market. Based on my 45 years in the market, it has had absolutely nothing to do with the economy. This is the reason why most of the advice you've received—that the economy is improving, that inventories are better, etc.—has had no impact on the market.

We have experienced a major historical psychological period similar to the 1650s tulip bulb mania in Holland and our own stock market in 1929. This has not been fully recognized by the Fed or most economists.

If you take the Nasdaq average from 1991 to the March 2000 top and then to its current low and lay it on top of the Dow Jones industrial average from 1921 to the 1929 top and its 1932 bottom, you'll see they're nearly identical. The only difference is that the last year of Wall Street's wild, unrestrained speculation in the Nasdaq's technology, Internet and biotech stocks was more excessive than the Dow's final 1929 binge.

Most Americans were invested in the bubble market of the late 1990s during the Clinton administration. They have lost 50% to 80% of their money because they didn't know how to manage risk and listened to poor advice. There is now an adverse supply demand situation at several large mutual funds that weighs on the market.

When you combine the extraordinary damage from the bursting of the tech bubble, the huge market losses that individual investors have suffered, the panicky liquidation of mutual fund holdings and the added psychological damage and fear from 9/11, history says recovery will be much slower and take much longer. For this reason, the economy needs more stimulus now than normal.

In return for giving Democrats what in their eyes amounts to a job creation bill, you could consider asking for another moderate, across-the-board income-tax cut for consumers only. The objection that Democrats will raise will be the deficit, which your team should be able to counter with some real historical research. I can help with five or six strong answers to deficit concerns, which I believe are overrated.

The Fed should surprise the stock market by lowering rates three-eighths of a percent to sustain our housing recovery and support flagging consumer and business confidence.

One last historical market observation: In early 1962, the SEC announced it was going to investigate the mutual fund industry. That scared the market, which began a sharp decline. Later, Kennedy rescinded a steel price increase, and the market really fell apart—even though nothing was wrong with the economy. Markets don't react well to uncertainty or prolonged government investigations.

If no new economic solutions are advanced and aggressively promoted by your administration, and if the news is dominated by government investigations and liberal critics, you could possibly lose Congress in November.

If you so desire, I would be happy to meet with you or any of your key policymakers to debate the above proposals.

Sincerely,

William J. O'Neil
Chairman and Founder

Paradoxically, the way to reduce government's capital gains income is to increase the capital gains rate and discourage everyone from taking gains or assuming additional risks. Currently, 50 percent of all stocks showing a profit that would be subject to a capital gains tax are never sold by their owners because they don't want to pay the tax. They stubbornly hold their stock for years or until death and thereby avoid paying any tax on their profit at all. So government unwittingly, through its somewhat empty-headed policy, always receives less capital gains tax revenue than if it would just simply cut the rates. Alan Greenspan has stated several times that a capital gains tax is one of the poorest ways to tax because it discourages investment and growth in our economy. The recently lowered capital gains rate of 15 percent proposed by the House Ways and Means Committee leader, Bill Thomas, of California, and included as part of the new tax cut package, will be a positive tax incentive for every investor in America.

We may have been of some small help in getting the capital gains rate lowered to 15 percent. Bill Thomas mentioned to one of our associates in a conversation around Christmas that he was aware of some of our suggestions and felt things like that might have a chance of making it through Congress since they had gained seats in the Senate in the November midterm elections. So, on January 2, I sent him a copy of a December 31, 2002, letter to the White House. The last few relevant paragraphs from that letter are as follows:

Allow $1500 of dividends tax-free and consider small business faster depreciation or more R&D tax breaks.

Exhibit 1: A sample of the 600 stocks that led new bull markets and economic recoveries in the last 50 years, America's greatest growth period.

They paid little in dividends, financed growth internally and by stock, not debt as academics assume. Eighty percent reduced debt as a percentage of equity or had no debt. A small number had stock buybacks. These happened early on and had nothing to do with later market excesses or malfeasance in 10 to 20 high-profile cases among 10,000 public stocks in the late 1990s.

Exhibit 2: America's important and essential older, large maintainer companies lost jobs from 1980 to 2000 while America gained 39 million jobs. Small business may have accounted for over 90 percent, if you add back SBs that jumped past 500 employees or were acquired and no longer counted as job creators.

My conclusion is cutting capital gains to 15 percent will create far more new companies, new jobs, and a stronger stock market and economy than ending double taxes on dividends could. It also means new small businesses created under paragraph 2 will pay only 7½ percent capital gains tax on long-term stock sold. That's a powerful, job-creating incentive worth dealing for.

After the head of the Senate Republicans entered into an agreement to limit any tax cut to 350 billion dollars and 3 Republican senators rebelled against larger tax cuts that would hurt the deficit, Bill Thomas wisely crafted an excellent plan with sunset provisions that preserved the vast majority of the president's plan and added the capital gain reduction.

It's additionally a myth that deficits by themselves cause higher inflation or interest rates, because there are many other more important factors at work that frequently override any possible negative effect of deficits. For example, deficits increased during the Reagan years, and inflation and interest rates fell consistently and dramatically year after year. Inflation, which stood at 11.8 percent when Reagan took office, had plunged to 4.5 percent by the time he left. The fed funds interest rate tumbled from 19.1 to 9.1. Meantime, the large military buildup that contributed to the deficits—the threat of our testing, developing, and deploying the Star Wars missile defense system—ultimately led to the defeat of the economically weak but militarily threatening Soviet Union. The tearing down of the Berlin Wall freed people who had been oppressed for 70 years. The end of the Cold War, in turn, permitted a builddown of defense, savings from which explain in large part the return of federal budget surpluses in the 1990s.

When people talk of our government's debt, they refer to only the debt side of our national balance sheet. No one ever calculates, thinks about, or talks about our government's total asset side, which in the last 50 years has increased more than the debt side. It's the debt-to-asset ratio that matters more than the debt level itself.

In the future, Congress should consider the possibility of reducing the holding period for capital gains to six months, which it was for many years. This will let our government collect needed taxes sooner. It will also create an added big incentive for people to invest.

More important, if we really want to improve the stock market and our economy's ability to create more jobs, the administration and Congress should seriously consider a simple, stripped-down version of the new small business creation plan proposed to President Bush in my July 2002 letter. The president clearly seemed to like it, but it was most likely shelved by his chief economic planner at the time, who designed and promoted his own agenda for the elimination of taxes on dividends. A strong incentive to create more new small businesses would be a backup insurance policy for our economy and our stock market. It would create new jobs, increase government's income by $39 billion over the first five years, and have no adverse effect on the deficit. Here's how a revised, simpler new small business and job creation plan could work:

Congress should agree to allow anyone who starts a brand-new small business (one that never existed before) employing at least three people to pay only one-half the new regular 15 percent capital gains rate on any stock or ownership sold by the founders or employees during the first 10 years in business. This will trigger a surge in small startups. Why? Because the small business creation plan means they would only be subject to a 7½ percent capital gains rate. It's the differential between a 35 percent top income tax bracket for new wannabe entrepreneurs and the low 7½ percent tax on long-term gains from creating and building a new venture that will be the inspiration for more risk takers to take the plunge and start new companies.

The expected result: an extra 100,000 new businesses and 530,000 new jobs (based on the past average of 5.3 employees for new small employer companies) in the first year alone. If the plan were kept in place for five years, our government would receive income taxes from the 366,667 net new businesses that were created over the life of the plan, as well as from the 2.855 million new job holders, each conservatively earning approximately $27,000. This assumes that only 50 percent of the new businesses survive five years, at which point they would each have roughly 11 employees, average sales of $600,000, and estimated profit margins of 13 percent.

These start-ups will buy furniture, equipment, supplies, and PCs; rent space; and hire accounting and other business services. These multiplier effects on the economy are not included in the above calculations.

A few simple rules may be needed to keep big companies from avoiding capital gains taxes by owning parts of the new firms and existing businesses from transferring assets to new ones. Basically, the incentive is for new companies that never existed before—brand-new start-ups.

I estimate that 1 percent of these new entrepreneurial firms will go public in a few years, helping revitalize and sustain our stock market and economy with 1000 badly needed innovative IPOs. (Currently there are few IPOs.) This program would cost the government absolutely nothing but would generate approximately $39 billion in added tax revenue over the first five years: $16.25 billion from the new firms paying corporate income tax plus $22.5 billion from individual tax returns from new job holders. It would also be a prudent hedge against the possibility of a slowly improving job recovery.

Since this new jobs creation program would be aimed strictly at the common man and woman, it should appeal to Democrats and Republicans alike. Both have a big stake in a strong recovery that they may not completely recognize. George W. Bush may be the president now, but he had barely taken office when the recession officially began, and it was during Bill Clinton's administration that the wild, anything-goes stock market bubble inflated and finally burst in February and March of 2000. Also, if a further terrorist attack occurs, it might possibly slow our recovery. These are risks we shouldn't take.

Now, if our government wants to really be bold and progressive with this Small Business Creation Act, it should allow new start-ups in all designated inner city minority or poverty areas to pay zero capital gains tax on any business interest the founding owners sell in their first 10 years in business. This would materially help inner city unemployment opportunities, especially among restless young people, and furthermore lead to a reduction in the crime rate.

What does all this have to do with the stock market? More new businesses create more jobs, a stronger economy, and therefore a more powerful, more sustainable stock market. I'll take that over slipping into another prolonged recession any day.

In conclusion, you now have in your hands a method and a time-tested, proven system with buy rules and sell rules that could just change your whole life.

The American dream goes on. There will be dozens of great new market leaders in every future bull market. The opportunities will be unlimited, but it's all up to you. It isn't easy, because you need to read and reread to get it all down. Repetition is how you learn any new skill—and investing successfully is a skill you can learn if you have the burning desire to work at it until you succeed. America truly is the land of opportunity for everyone.

APPENDIX A

How to Use the CAN SLIM Approach to Screen for Growth Stocks

By John Bajkowski

Take an attention-grabbing book title, toss in an easy-to-remember acronym, and top it off with a daily business newspaper that supplies information required for preliminary analysis: You've got the recipe for a popular investment strategy. The CAN SLIM approach is presented by William O'Neil, publisher of *Investor's Business Daily,* in his book titled *How to Make Money in Stocks: A Winning System in Good Times or Bad.*

The second edition of *How to Make Money in Stocks* presented a stock selection approach developed by studying 500 of the biggest stock market winners from 1953 to 1993. The CAN SLIM approach presented in the book was based upon the characteristics that these winning stocks possessed prior to their big price run-ups. Recently, O'Neil extended his analysis of past market winners to 600 companies that performed strongly from 1953 to 2001 and revised a number of CAN SLIM criteria. The third edition of *How to Make Money in Stocks* was published last year and presents the revised CAN SLIM rules (see Table

John Bajkowski is AAII's financial analysis vice president and editor of *Computerized Investing.* Reprinted by *Investor's Business Daily* with Permission (c) AAII 2003.

Table A.1 Revised CAN SLIM Rules

	Third edition	Comparison to second edition
	C = current quarterly earnings per share: the higher, the better	
Primary factors	• Should show a major percentage increase (18% or 20% minimum) in the current quarterly EPS when compared to the prior year's same quarter.	Same as in second edition
	• Omit a company's one-time extraordinary gains.	Same as in second edition
	• Look for accelerating quarterly earnings growth.	Same as in second edition
Secondary factors	• Look for quarterly sales growth of 25% or at least an acceleration in rate of sales percentage improvements over the last three quarters.	New to third edition
	• Find at least one other stock in the same group showing strong quarterly earnings growth.	Same as in second edition
	A = annual earnings increases: look for significant growth	
Primary factors	• The annual compounded growth rate for EPS should be at least 25%.	The EPS annual compounded growth rate should be at least 25% over the last four or five years.
	• Significant growth in EPS for each of the last three years.	Each year's annual EPS for the last five years should show an increase over the prior year's earnings.
Secondary factors	• The consensus earnings estimate for the next year should be higher than the current year.	Same as in second edition
	• Return on equity of 17% or more.	New to third edition
	• Look for annual cash flow per share greater than actual earnings per share by at least 20%.	New to third edition
	• Earnings should be stable and consistent from year to year over the last three years.	Earnings should be stable and consistent from year to year over the last five years.

	N = new products, new management, new highs: buying at the right time	
Primary factors	• Look for companies with a major new product or service, new management, or a positive change for the industry.	Same as in second edition
Secondary factors	• Look for stocks close to or making new highs in price after a period of consolidation. • Strong volume on price move up.	Same as in second edition
	S = Supply and demand: shares outstanding plus big volume demand	
Primary factors	• Any size stock can be purchased under the CAN SLIM system. • The market will shift its emphasis between small- and large-cap stocks over time.	Stocks with a small or reasonable number of shares outstanding will, other things being equal, usually outperform older, large-capitalization stocks.
	• When choosing between two stocks, the stock with the lower number of shares should perform better to the upside, but can come down just as fast.	Greater emphasis on stocks with limited float in second edition.
Secondary factors	• Stocks with a large percentage of ownership by top management are generally good prospects.	Same as in second edition
	• Look for companies buying their own stock in the open market.	Same as in second edition
	• Look for companies with a lower debt-to-equity ratio and companies reducing their debt-to-equity ratios over the last few years.	Same as in second edition

(Continued)

Table A.1 Revised CAN SLIM Rules (*Continued*)

	Third edition	Comparison to second edition
	L = leader or laggard: which is your stock?	
Primary Factors	• Buy among the top two or three stocks in a strong industry group.	Same as in second edition
	• Use relative price strength to separate the leaders from the laggards—a stock with a relative strength rank below 70% is lagging and should be avoided.	Same as in second edition
Secondary factors	• Look for companies with a relative strength rank of 80% or higher that are in a chart base pattern.	Same as in second edition, but greater emphasis on limiting buys to stocks with a relative strength rank of 80% or greater in third edition.
	• Don't buy stocks with weaker than average performance during a market correction.	Same as in second edition
	I = institutional sponsorship: follow the leaders	
Primary factors	• Look for a stock to have several institutional owners. 10 might be a reasonable minimum.	Same as in second edition
	• Look at quality of owners—seek out stocks held by at least one or two savvy portfolio managers.	Same as in second edition
	• Look for stocks with an increasing, not decreasing, number of sponsors.	Same as in second edition
Secondary factors	• Avoid stocks that are over-owned—excessive institutional ownership.	Same as in second edition

M = market direction		
Primary factors	• It is difficult to fight the trend, so try to determine if you are in a bull or bear market.	Same as in second edition
	• Follow and understand what the general market averages are doing every day.	Same as in second edition
	• Try to go 25% into cash when the market peaks and begins a major reversal.	Same as in second edition
	• Heavy volume without significant price progress may signal a top, but initial market decline may be on lower volume.	Same as in second edition
Secondary factors	• Follow market leaders for clues on strength of market.	Same as in second edition
	• Look for divergence of key averages and indexes at major turns—divergence points to weaker and narrow market movement.	Same as in second edition
	• Sentiment indicators may help highlight extreme psychological reversal points.	Same as in second edition
	• The change in the discount rate is a valuable indicator to watch as a confirmation of market moves.	Same as in second edition

145

A.1). This article presents the CAN SLIM approach with an eye toward the recent changes and its application using AAII's stock screening system—*Stock Investor Pro.* Additionally, the March/April 2003 issue of *Computerized Investing* presents how to apply the CAN SLIM stock screen using Internet stock screening systems.

CAN SLIM Overview

The CAN SLIM approach seeks companies with a proven record of quarterly and annual earnings and sales growth showing strong relative price strength and support from leading institutions. O'Neil does not mind paying rich premiums for stocks with good prospects. He feels that most strategies seeking stocks with low price-earnings are flawed because they ignore the price trend determining the price-earnings ratio, as well as the quality of the underlying earnings within the ratio. O'Neil believes that stocks generally sell for what they are worth and most stocks with low price-earnings ratios are probably priced correctly by the market. O'Neil also asserts that it is important to follow the market closely and try to lighten up your stock exposure when going into a bear market.

C = Current Quarterly Earnings

The CAN SLIM approach focuses on companies with proven records of earnings growth that are still in a stage of earnings acceleration. O'Neil's study of winning stocks revealed that these securities generally had strong quarterly earnings per share performance prior to their significant price run-ups.

O'Neil recommends looking for stocks with a minimum increase in quarterly earnings of 18 percent to 20 percent over the same quarterly period one year ago. When screening for quarterly earnings increases, it is important to compare a quarter to the equivalent quarter last year—in other words, this year's second quarter compared to last year's second quarter. Many firms have seasonal patterns to their earnings, and comparing similar quarters helps to take this into account.

Another item to watch for when screening for percentage changes is a meaningless figure created by having a very small base number. For example, an increase from one penny to 10 cents translates into a 900 percent earnings increase. It is always advisable to look at the raw numbers of the company passing the screen. This allows you to gauge the overall trend and stability in earnings and other items such as sales and cash flow.

Whenever you are working with earnings, the issue of how to handle extraordinary earnings comes into play. One-time events can distort the actual trend in earnings and make the company performance look better or worse than a comparison against a firm without special charges. O'Neil recommends excluding these nonrecurring items from the analysis.

The first two screens require quarterly earnings growth greater than or equal to 20 percent and positive earnings per share from continuing operations for the current quarter. We used *Stock Investor Pro,* with data as of March 14, 2003, for the screen. Only 2343 stocks out of an initial universe of 8428 met these two criteria.

Beyond looking for strong quarterly growth, O'Neil likes to see an increasing rate of growth. An increasing rate of growth in quarterly earnings per share is so important in the CAN SLIM system that O'Neil warns shareholders to consider selling holdings of companies that show a slowing rate of growth for two quarters in a row. The next screen specified that the earnings growth rate from the quarter one year ago compared to the latest quarter be higher than a similar quarter one year earlier. This reduced the number of passing companies to 1556.

As a confirmation of the quarterly earnings screen, O'Neil likes to see same-quarter growth in sales greater than 25 percent or at least accelerating over the last three quarters. This new screening requirement was added to the third edition of O'Neil's book and seeks to help confirm the quality of a firm's earnings. Independently, 3647 stocks have a current quarterly sales growth greater than or equal to 25 percent, but combined with the other filters the number of passing companies was reduced to 393.

The CAN SLIM system is not purely mechanical and O'Neil also likes to find at least one other stock in the same industry group that shows strong quarterly earnings growth as confirmation that the industry is strong.

A = Annual Earnings Increases

Winning stocks in O'Neil's study had a steady and significant record of annual earnings in addition to a strong record of current earnings. O'Neil's primary screen for annual earnings increases requires that earnings per share show an increase in each of the last three years. This filter has been loosened slightly from the prior edition, which required earnings increases over each of the last five years.

In applying this screen in *Stock Investor Pro*, we specified that earnings per share from continuing operations be higher for each year when compared against the previous year. To help guard against any recent reversal in trend, a criterion was included requiring that earnings over the last 12 months be greater than or equal to earnings from the latest fiscal year. When screened by itself, 795 companies passed this filter compared to the 469 companies that passed the second edition's tighter filter. Adding the filter requiring a year-by-year earnings increase for each of the last three years to the current growth filters reduced the passing number of companies to just 60 stocks. This is not surprising given the economic environment over the last few years.

O'Neil also recommends screening for companies showing a strong annual growth rate of 25 percent over the last three years. This filter only cut an additional six stocks, which is to be expected given the strict consistent year-by-year growth requirement.

Optimally, the consensus earnings estimate for the next year should be higher than the latest reported year. Adding this filter reduced the number of passing companies to 39. When working with consensus earnings estimates it is important to remember that only the larger and more active firms will have analysts tracking them and providing estimates. About half of the stocks in *Stock Investor Pro* have consensus earnings estimates, so this filter will also tend to screen out micro-cap stocks.

Another potential addition to the CAN SLIM screen is a requirement for high return on equity (ROE: net income divided by shareholder's equity). O'Neil's studies showed that the greatest winning stocks had ROEs of at least 17 percent. O'Neil uses this measure to separate well-managed companies from poorly managed ones. Adding this filter would have reduced the number of passing companies to 19 from 39. Our testing over the last five years revealed that this requirement often led to a very small number of passing stocks and hurt performance since 2001. The revised screen does not make use of the return on equity filter.

N = New Products, New Management, New Highs

O'Neil feels that a stock needs a catalyst to start a strong price advance. In his study of winning stocks, he found that 95 percent of the winning stocks had some sort of fundamental spark to push the company ahead of the pack. This catalyst can be a new product or service, a new management team employed after a period of lackluster performance, or even a structural change in a company's industry—such as a new technology.

These are very qualitative factors that do not lend themselves easily to screening. A second consideration that O'Neil emphasizes is that investors should pursue stocks showing strong upward price movement. O'Neil says that stocks that seem too high-priced and risky most often go even higher, while stocks that seem cheap often go even lower. Stocks that are making the new high list while accompanied by a big increase in volume might be prospects worth checking. A stock making a new high after undergoing a period of price correction and consolidation is especially interesting.

O'Neil's newspaper, *Investor's Business Daily*, highlights stocks within 10 percent of their 52-week high and this was the criterion established for the screen. One would expect many companies to pass during a strong market expansion, while a smaller number of companies would pass during a declining market. Given the weak market during the first few months of 2003, it is not surprising that adding this filter reduced the number of passing companies from 39 to 4. As of March 14, 2003, a total of 1037 stocks out of a universe of 8428 were trading within 10 percent of their 52-week high.

S = Supply and Demand

O'Neil emphasized smaller-capitalization stocks more strongly in his earlier editions. The third edition states that any size stock can be purchased using the CAN SLIM approach, but smaller companies will be more volatile with greater pop to the upside and downside. Companies buying back their stock on the open market are preferred, as well as companies with management stock ownership. No definitive screens now come out of the S element of the CAN SLIM system, but Table A.1 identifies a number of factors to consider when analyzing passing companies.

L = Leader or Laggard

O'Neil is not a patient value investor looking for out-of-favor companies and willing to wait for the market to come around to his viewpoint. Rather, he prefers to identify rapidly growing companies that are market leaders in rapidly expanding industries. O'Neil advocates buying among the best two or three stocks in a group. He feels that you will be compensated for any premium you pay for these leaders with significantly higher rates of return.

O'Neil suggests using relative strength to identify market leaders. Relative strength compares the performance of a stock relative to the market as a whole. Relative strength is reported in many ways and you must be careful to understand how the relative strength figure is used in a given screening system.

Companies are often ranked by their price performance for a given period of time and their percentage ranking among all stocks is calculated to show the relative position against other stocks. *Investor's Business Daily* presents the percentage ranking of stocks and O'Neil recommends avoiding any stock with relative strength rank below 70 percent and only seeking out stocks with a percentage rank of 80 percent or better—stocks that have performed better than 80 percent of all stocks. While only about 1680 firms (8428 × 20%) have a 52-week relative strength rank of 80 percent or greater, this filter did not further reduce the number of passing companies. In the market environment at the time of the screen, the price as a percent of a 52-week high proved to be a more stringent price strength screen.

I = Institutional Sponsorship

O'Neil feels that a stock needs a few institutional sponsors for it to show above-market performance. Ten institutional owners is suggested as a reasonable minimum number. This number refers to actual institutional owners of the common stock, not institutional analysts tracking and providing earnings estimates on stocks.

Beyond looking for a minimum number of institutional owners, O'Neil suggests that investors study the recent record of the institutions. The analysis of the holdings of successful mutual funds represents a good resource for the individual investor because of the widely distributed information on mutual funds. Web sites such as Morningstar.com (www.morningstar.com) and CNBC on MSN Money (moneycentral.msn.com/investor) disclose the top mutual funds that own a given stock.

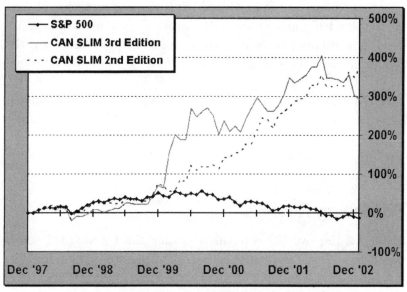

Figure A.1 CAN SLIM Performance
(*Source: AAII's* Stock Investor Pro)

The next filter required a minimum of 10 institutional shareholders. About 5500 stocks pass this filter independently. Adding it to the CAN SLIM filter in *Stock Investor Pro* did not cut any additional stocks.

O'Neil also likes to see the number of institutional shareholders increasing for a given stock in the most recent quarters. *Stock Investor Pro* does not report the number of institutional shareholders over time, but it does report on number of shares sold and purchased by institutions over the last quarter. Our last filter specified that the number of shares purchased should be greater than or equal to the number of shares sold by institutions over the last quarter. This filter did not further reduce the number of passing stocks, which are shown in Table A.2.

M = Market Direction

The final aspect of the CAN SLIM system looks at the overall market direction. While it does not impact the selection of specific stocks, the trend of the overall market will have a tremendous impact on the performance of your portfolio. O'Neil tends to focus on technical measures when determining the overall direction of the marketplace. Any good technical program or Web site, or even *Investor's Business Daily,* should provide you with the necessary tools to study market movement.

O'Neil finds it difficult to fight the trend, so it is important to determine if you are in a bull or bear market. Table A.1 summarizes the type of factors that O'Neil considers when trying to gauge market strength.

Screening Results

Table A.2 displays the companies passing the CAN SLIM screen based upon our interpretation of the rules presented in both the third and the second editions of O'Neil's book.

Four stocks passed the third edition screen compared to the two passing the second edition screen. This is actually a reversal of the nor-

Table A.2 Stocks That Passed the CAN SLIM Screen

Company (Exchange: Ticker)	EPS grth. last qtr. vs. yr. ago (%)	EPS grth. prior qtr. vs. yr. ago (%)	Sales grth. last qtr. vs. yr. ago (%)	Annual EPS grth. rate (3-yr.) (%)	Long-term EPS grth. est. (%)	Price as % of 52-wk. high (%)	52-wk. rel. strgth. rank (%)	Inst'l. share holders (no.)	Net inst'l. shares purch. (1000s)	Description
				Third edition CAN SLIM screen						
Apollo Group, Inc (M: APOL)	72.2	50.0	35.4	37.8	24.3	99	93	1142	6126	Adult higher ed.
FTI Consulting, Inc (N: FCN)	192.3	53.3	91.4	36.7	21.0	95	94	384	2005	Consulting firm
International Game Tech (N: IGT)	42.3	10.8	76.4	70.5	17.3	97	88	980	2102	Casino gaming prods.
Teva Pharmaceutical Indus (M: TEVA)	73.3	20.0	35.8	49.9	23.8	95	91	942	11210	Major theraputic drugs
				Second Edition CAN SLIM Screen						
Commercial Bankshares (M: CLBK)	30.0	28.2	-3.2	16.0	8.0	96	94	27	21	Bank holding co.
Oshkosh Truck Corporation (N: OSK)	28.8	-3.8	17.9	13.1	15.9	90	76	383	-121	Specialty trucks

Exchange Key: N = New York Stock Exchange
M = Nasdaq National or Small-Cap Markets

Statistics are based on figures as of March 14, 2003.

mal pattern. We have backtested the revised third edition screen and have found that, on average, five stocks passed this screen every month compared to 12 stocks passing the second edition screen on a monthly basis from December 1997 through March 2003. As many as 32 stocks have passed the second edition screen, while the greatest number of stocks passing the third edition screen was 15 over this time period. On three occasions, no stocks passed the third edition screen, while as little as one stock has passed the second edition screen.

Although it is difficult to draw conclusions with such a small sample, the stocks passing the third edition screen tend to be larger companies held by more institutional owners, with stronger quarterly earnings and sales growth as well as stronger historical and expected annual earnings growth.

We have been testing the performance of a wide range of screening systems for over five years now and our interpretation of the CAN SLIM approach has proven to be one of the most consistent and strongest-performing screens during both bull and bear markets. Figure A.1 provides a quick view of the initial testing of the revised CAN SLIM approach. The revised approach has proven to be a bit more volatile—rising higher and faster in the bull market of the late 1990s but then giving up its lead in the recent bear market. Both strategies will be tracked and reported on in the Stock Screens area of AAII.com as well as the semiannual review of strategies in the *AAII Journal.*

Conclusion

The CAN SLIM system has great appeal to the active investor looking for growth stocks. While the approach is specific, it also stresses the art of investing when interpreting the direction of the market. Here we have touched upon CAN SLIM rules helpful in identifying promising stocks. It is important to keep in mind that ideas from a computer screen merely represent a starting point that requires further analysis before action.

Data Source: AAII's *Stock Investor Pro*/Market Guide, Inc. and I/B/E/S.

APPENDIX B

All About CAN SLIM

Here is a summary of CAN SLIM as taught in the three editions of *How to Make Money in Stocks: 24 Essential Lessons to Investment Success* and IBD's many all-day paid workshops that have been attended by tens of thousands of serious investors.

C = Current Quarterly Earnings per Share

They must be up at least 18 to 20 percent as a minimum and show recent acceleration in their percentage rate of quarterly increases. The average percent increase in current quarterly earnings of all great winners for the last 50 years was 70 percent. The very best showed earnings increases of 100 to 200 percent. Price-to-earnings (P/E) ratios were proven to *not* be a cause of outstanding stock performance, but rather an end effect or end result of excellent and improving earnings and sales increases. P/E ratios of the best-performing stocks each year for the past half-century were higher than those of the market indexes and these individual stock P/Es significantly expanded as their superior-performing companies, at the time, continued their period of improving earnings and sales. Companies with five to seven quarters in a row of earnings up a meaningful amount were most dependable. The findings and conclusions from our 50-year scientific study of all variables in successful companies were the opposite of the way virtually all fundamental Wall Street research has operated over the years and what other national business newspapers have believed in the past.

(Above-average P/Es have been generally regarded as too high, and if they increased, stocks were downgraded, recommended to be avoided, or sold. Later, after a stock finally topped and the P/E declined, they were, in many cases, recommended as holds or good buys. This explains to a degree why so much money can be lost listening to some analysts' recommendations, whether they appear on TV market programs, in written research reports, or in certain respected national business newspapers as support for strong opinion pieces or even attack articles. These attack articles are usually designed to tear into a company, cause selling in stock, and knock its price down based solely on the publication's opinion that the stock's P/E seems too high.)

A = Annual Earning per Share

This should show growth in each of the past three years. The annual growth rate can vary from 25 percent to as much as 250 percent or more. Either the annual pretax profit margin or annual return on equity should be expanding. Return or equity (ROE) should be 17 percent or higher. The best companies usually show ROE of 20 to 50 percent or more. Consensus earnings estimates for the next year should also be up a reasonable amount.

Note: IBD's proprietary EPS Rating is a combination of each company's three-year earnings growth rate and the last few quarters' earnings growth. It can be found in IBD's daily stock tables and Daily Graphs charts.

N = Buy Stocks with Superior New Products, New Services, or New Management or Major New Improvements in Industry Conditions

Many may be newer entrepreneurial companies that had IPOs recently or in the previous 10 years. Use charts to buy these stocks as they begin to emerge from sound chart base patterns of seven weeks or more and are at proper buy points. These correct buy points will be at or within 10 to 15 percent of new price highs for the year. At the buy point, trading volume for the day should increase 50 percent or more above the stock's average daily volume. If the stock advances 2 or 3 percent from your initial buy price, follow up with a smaller add-on buy. All buying should be limited to the stock's initial 5 percent move up from its buy point. On the other hand, any and all stocks that decline 7 percent below the price you paid must be sold (with no exceptions) to cut short all of your losses and prevent the possibility of eventually having several substantially larger, seriously damaging losses in your portfolio. (Investors who lose large amounts of money simply do not follow this vital, time-tested, and proven CAN SLIM protection rule of cutting short all of their losses.)

S = Supply and Demand

This involves shares outstanding plus big volume demand. Any size stock can be bought under the CAN SLIM method. Smaller-capitalization stocks may perform better, but are more volatile and can come down just as fast as they go up. Stocks with ownership management or companies buying back their own stock in the open market are preferred. Monitor the demand for shares by checking the percentage change in volume for each of your stocks in IBD's stock tables and day-to-day price and volume changes on Daily Graphs' daily charts.

L = Leaders or Laggards

Concentrate your buying in the top two or three rated stocks in one of the strongest 10 or 15 of the 197 Industry Groups. Avoid stocks with a Relative Strength Rating below 70, and concentrate on those rated 80 and higher that are in a sound chart base pattern. A company should be number one in its particular field or industry in terms of annual earnings growth, sales growth, pretax and after-tax profit margins, return on equity, and product quality. You are looking to buy really great companies that are the very best fundamentally and in market price and volume behavior, not just one without the other. Sell off your laggard, worst-performing stocks.

I = Institutional Sponsorship

You always want good institutional sponsors behind every stock you buy—at least 25 or more institutional owners. That's because mutual funds are the big movers of stocks due to the size of their purchases. The number of mutual funds owning your stock should be increasing for each of the last several quarters. This data is provided in IBD and Daily Graphs.

A few of the smarter, better-performing mutual funds should have purchased the stocks in the previous quarter. Even if the data available to you is many weeks after a fund's reporting period, it is of value. Fund sponsorship is an important fundamental measurement, because most funds will not purchase a company until they've checked it out and believe the story and fundamentals to be sound. They do not tend to buy cheap, low-priced, low-quality, or lower-grade companies that have poor backing, poor marketability, or a questionable record.

However, you do not buy just any stock the fund has bought, because they also make many mistakes or buy some mediocre performers, just as you have probably done in the past. You buy only the best ones the fund owns that fit every one of your time-tested CAN SLIM rules.

That's why analyzing daily and weekly charts' price and volume action is crucial to outstanding success, because once you learn to do this with some practice and skill, it can tell you if your stock is under accumulation by professional or institutional sponsors or not, and when is a more correct time to begin your purchasing. Most amateur investors, critics, cynics, and many university professors simply do not understand all of this, and that's why most are not highly successful when investing in the stock market. The N, I, and M are the most underestimated, least understood elements in the CAN SLIM method by 95 percent of all investors.

M = Market Direction

You must learn to follow and correctly interpret a daily price and volume chart of the major stock market indexes every day if you want to know when a new major uptrend is starting or the market is topping and starting what could become the beginning of a serious correction or major new bear market. Lack of this skill or knowledge is why 98 percent of investors got hurt in the 2000 to 2002 market.

Why are the market indexes so critical? Because, when the key general market indexes top and turn down, three out of four of your stocks will sooner or later follow and many can drop percentage-wise much more than the indexes.

Study IBD's "General Market" page and read IBD's "Big Picture" column on interpreting the general market everyday. People who paid strict attention to it sold or raised significant cash in March 2000 and were able to protect themselves. Learn to recognize follow-through days for market bottoms and distribution days for market tops in the key indexes. Also, it's vitally important to understand selling rules that tell you when market leaders are topping since this is another way of recognizing the top in a general market. Listening to personal opinions and feelings is of no value and can be exceedingly damaging at key market points.

The reason CAN SLIM works so well when all of its seven steps are put together and carefully followed is that it is based solely on meticulous research into how the market has worked, cycle after cycle, for the last 50 years. In other words, it is not my system, but a history of how the market realistically has worked rather than how most people think it works. If any of the CAN SLIM steps are neglected, your results will suffer. It's the combination of all of the seven key factors together that creates real success. It's analogous to tennis. You can't just hit a good forehand shot and expect to win. You also have to have a good backhand, a lob shot, an overhead shot, a midcourt volley, a good first serve, and a good second serve that is different from your first serve.

APPENDIX C

Market Memo

March 17, 2003

Over the previous 21 days we observed what we believed to be a bottom-building process in that 13 days of accumulation occurred in the NASDAQ, the de facto leading index, as it was in the process of moving toward its recent low. This has now been confirmed by today's follow-through day on all market indexes.

We believe the market has successfully retested its October 2002 low by pulling back to a level just above the October low and undercutting the recent February 13, 2003 low. This represents a logical pull-back area for the market, and we believe the stage is now set for an improving market environment. This recent undercut also represented the third wave down from the December 2, 2002 peak on all the major market indexes. We note the NASDAQ attempted to rally above its 200-day moving average three times and failed each time. After three such rally failures convinced many to be negative, the psychology has now shifted and the NASDAQ appears to be succeeding in what is now its fourth attempt to rally above this moving average— a positive sign, in our view.

We believe the war in Iraq will ultimately be a positive for the market, and will cause terrorist sponsor states to rethink their associations with and support of terrorism. Furthermore, the resolution of the Iraqi crisis should aid in the expansion of free markets and democracy in that region, continuing the "super trend" of more and more countries moving toward democracy and free markets that began with the fall of the Berlin Wall. The change in the current Iraqi regime should also contribute to a better flow of oil from the region, resulting in lower oil prices and providing a boost to the U.S. economy. Resolution of the crisis will also bolster consumer confidence. This could have a further effect on increasing the "political capital" of the Bush Administration, enabling the passage of their economic stimulus package with minor revisions.

We believe that negative factors in the market have run out of time, and that the three-year bear market has served to create reasonable valuations for companies that are leaders in their field, have superior products and services, and are showing 8, 10, 12, or more quarters in a row of strong earnings growth. For specific ideas, clients should refer to our *New Stock Market Ideas* and *Big-Cap Index Plus* equity idea services.

William J. O'Neil
Chairman

> A rare market memo sent to William O'Neil + Co.'s 600 institutional accounts only at key turning points.

APPENDIX D

Testimonials for *The Successful Investor*

Richard Hampton: I am a working-class person. Just a regular joe in a machine shop. I had invested with a firm to secure the college money for my four children and some retirement money. Three years ago I saw the money I accumulated go from nearly $70,000 to less than $12,000. I took the remaining money to a larger, more reliable firm. I saw good growth for over a year, then saw this amount go down to nearly $5000.

Nearly nine months ago I started reading your paper from front to back using the computer dictionary to learn the terms. I especially utilized the Stock Checkup on investors.com as a standard for selection. I took $3,000 and now am up to $14,000 and feel very secure and in control for the first time with my investments. Maybe I am just lucky, but I followed your information to the letter.

I believe in your paper and would recommend it to anyone. It is easy for me to understand compared to some others I have purchased. I learned that no one really cares about the small investor, so you have to keep an eye on your own investments. A small investor like me has to have access to information that is easy to understand. Your paper and online service have provided me with all of this. All you have to do is take the time, learn how to use it, and do just that.

Dennis Coleman: As a convinced student of your philosophy, I have followed your rules and IBD wholeheartedly for over three years and I cannot thank you enough for my improved capital gains.

Ruth Battey: I got started in the market in 1990 after reading *How to Make Money in Stocks,* and what it did for me is truly unbelievable. You really explain every aspect of the market so well. I also have been a subscriber of the *Investor's Business Daily* since that year and I spend two hours per day on it. Thanks for helping to make me secure in my investments.

Keith Baldwin: Thank you for providing an efficient newspaper that educates, inspires, and provides data for investors to make their own decisions.

Jonathan Goodwin: IBD has been a part of my life for the last 10 years. I think it's the best paper I've ever seen. It's changed the way I think about money. It saved me a bundle at the peak of 2000. I'm looking at retiring in five years, and I'd say that 75 percent of that is due to the paper.

Michael Burton: I am a mentor to a child who has no dad. I have met with him weekly for three years. I use the "Leaders & Success" column to develop messages for him that he can apply to his benefit. That this is working is no surprise, I am sure, for as we think, so we are. But now that several of his friends have joined us in these discussions it has been doubly gratifying. Thanks for your positive contribution to these kids' lives.

Annette O'Connor: During the last three months I have taken the highlighted stocks from your newspaper each day and put them into my Quicken portfolio. I have found these stocks to have done very well due to the fundamentals that Mr. O'Neil teaches. I have also purchased a number of these stocks after doing some research and looking at charts on your Web site. I have a long way to go in fully understanding charts, but the money I spend for your paper is well worth it.

I listen to CNBC and other news stations regarding stocks and by far your advice in your newspaper is superior in every way.

I also have followed the sell advice, which if I had been more conscious of it a couple of years ago, I would not have lost nearly the money that I did.

Thank you, thank you!

Scott St. Clair: I would have to say that IBD and *How to Make Money in Stocks* have allowed me the kind of financial freedom that very few are lucky enough to have. I started as a broker/investor in 1995 using O'Neil's system. Not only did it allow me to make triple-digit gains up until 2000, but [it allowed me to] keep those gains by helping me to recognize the massive top in the market that year. (I had my best year in 2000 by being short for most of the year.) When the bull market resumes, I know that these tools will keep me focused in the best stocks.

Randy Stotts: I have just started using IBD and I finally have some decent information to base my future buying and selling habits on. Your *SmartSelect*® Ratings make it easy to pick solid companies and stay clear of the weak ones. Thanks for giving me the tools to get started back in the right direction. I feel I have a fighting chance now.

Richard Youngblood: Just want to say thanks to Bill O'Neil and IBD for the system of investing that you teach. The concepts of only buying stocks when they break out of bases during market uptrends, and quickly cutting losses is a lifesaver in a bear market such as this one. Lately, I have found few if any buying opportunities and, therefore, my capital has remained safe on the sidelines. I only wish I had fully adopted your methods for my investing years ago. I look forward to being able to again use CAN SLIM in a good market. Thanks again.

Gregg Rainone: IBD is indispensable, and William O'Neil is arguably *the* leading educator regarding the stock market in the modern era. His contribution to the public in the marketplace has been huge, bordering on the philanthropic, actually.

Checking the "Big Picture" page, and other related data in IBD, on a daily basis is mandatory for operating in the markets.

Barbara James: I cannot afford *not* to have IBD, Daily Graphs Online and Industry Groups on a daily basis. Thank you to everyone at IBD for the wealth of information and knowledge you pass on to an amateur investor such as I.

Grey Hall: A little over one year ago I bought *24 Essential Lessons for Investment Success* by Bill O'Neil. I timidly invested $5000 into the stock market, doubling it in my first year of learning and trading by using his guidance.

My second year began this month and by the 16th, my portfolio is up 24 percent. This latest surge coincides with my subscription to IBD and investors.com and is no doubt a result of the discipline instilled in me by these incredible tools. My original hesitance has turned to complete confidence that I can make the choices necessary to steadily increase the net worth of my portfolio.

Thanks; and for those small investors who don't know where to turn to for advice . . . it doesn't get any better than this!

Randy Mcelhanon: I heard about IBD from a friend in October of 2001. I had recently purchased shares of WorldCom at $15.00 a share. After reviewing my positions on your stock profiles I recognized that WorldCom should be liquidated immediately. I sold at $15.00 a share in lieu of the current price of 15 cents.

Thank you, IBD!

I hate to think where I would be if I had not heard about IBD. In the last eight months, IBD has taught me how to make money in the stock market, and I'm excited about what I can accomplish when we begin a new bull market!

Eric Martins: Your paper rules! I have saved thousands by staying out of the market while all of my friends and family hold and fold. Since learning to utilize technical analysis, I have stayed clear of several losers. I have also sold off stocks from sectors that were performing poorly according to your industry rankings.

Keep up the good work. I have recommended your paper to numerous people.

Kim Parkhurst: Just a word of praise: I'm a beginning investor who knew nothing about the stock market three weeks ago and had never invested a dime. Through Bill O'Neil's *How to Make Money in Stocks: 24 Essential Lessons for Investment Success,* and the excellent coverage, education, and tips provided in IBD and its Web site, I find myself more knowledgeable than most people I know who've been investing (and losing money) for years. Thank you and keep up the great work!

Porter J. Leaman: The CAN SLIM method really does work. I think of IBD as a research tool for companies with superior fundamentals and then use technical analysis on [IBD's] weekly and daily charts to buy at the most optimum time. Thank you, Mr. O'Neil for publishing IBD. It can really help investors learn to be smart investors instead of listening to CNBC.

Mike Goode: *Investor's Business Daily* has helped me make money. I've about doubled the performance that I've had previously. One of the reasons I really like *Investor's Business Daily* is because you do start seeing and noticing stocks move 200 percent and 300 percent and a whole bunch that moved 100 percent. I'm very excited about CAN SLIM. This investment philosophy has really helped me to avoid making a lot of mistakes that are very common with almost every investor. You really have to watch for all seven criteria of CAN SLIM. I would tell anyone ready to get started to read the book *How to Make Money in Stocks,* look at the charts in the book, and then keep reading the book over and over again.

Robert J. Furlan: I'm 33 years old and I've been a subscriber to IBD for about 11 years (since 1990). I subscribed to the WSJ when I was in college, but after graduating I took the two-week trial for IBD. My life changed then. I started using IBD's principles and it just clicked. Needless to say, I dropped the WSJ permanently and IBD became my bible. Soon my friends and family were asking if I could pick stocks for them. So that led me to start an investment partnership in August 1994 with my partner. We were CPAs who worked at the same accounting firm. We used to read IBD and talk about stocks on our lunch hour. We started with about $15,000 and now have over $2 million with over 30 investors. We have retired from being CPAs and work full-time on investments. The year 2000 was an especially breakout year for us as our fund was up over 40 percent versus the markets being down so huge. We had all the popular tech stocks (the ones that made money) but because of IBD we knew how to sell. We sold tech stocks over $200 that are now trading at $10 and we never got fooled into trying to buy these stocks on the way down. If one properly followed all of IBD's principles, crucial word being *all*, one should never have been caught in the bloodbath. I figure I've made more money in stocks using Bill O'Neil's principles and IBD with Daily Graphs as my daily resources than I've made as a CPA over the last 10 years. And now I get to do my true passion full-time for the rest of my life and get very rich in the process. However, I would truly not know what to do if I didn't have IBD, so it certainly is worth gold to me.

Adrian Mcgeedy: If you want to come to the investment world, *Investor's Business Daily* is the only worthwhile vehicle I've come across that will protect you and keep you afloat.

Veera Reddy: I want to share my success story because I'm the biggest fan of IBD and William O'Neil in a short period of time.

When I first came to the U.S. from India in May 2000 I didn't have any strategy in investing. I plunged into the markets after two months. I bought a basket of tech stocks like Cisco, Nortel Networks, JDSU, Intel, etc., with the opinions of friends and coworkers. But the sad part is, I lost more than 50 percent of my portfolio because I didn't know the fundamental rule of selling. To gain knowledge in investing I tried a lot of Web sites, but nothing was very educational.

Then I came across IBD. I liked the paper and got a subscription to it. I read the book by O'Neil, *24 Essential Lessons for Investment Success,* and I treat it as my investment bible. I got the grasp of buying at breakouts but am still learning the sell rules.

I love the "Leaders & Success" section, as it gives inspiration to me to go ahead in my life and think about life in a positive and successful way.

IBD is really one of my greatest addictions.

Kelly Caudle: My husband and I started using IBD several months ago. Since then, even in this volatile market, we have made money. We have most of our money in cash right now because of the market volatility. The IBD was so on target when all the other financial advisors were telling and begging people to get back in! IBD is the *only* paper that was saying to exercise caution and to probably stay out. Keep up the good work!

Jim Elder: "Leaders & Success" is an important part of my mornings. It is an inspirational tool that I utilize not only to ensure that I begin my days on a positive note, but it gives me food for thought on how it can improve my life. I also share most of them with my college-age kids to let them know that most successful people started out as average people, just like them.

Steve Gardels: My wife and I were only able to invest in mutual funds in our IRAs and 401ks. We stayed in growth funds for years, thanks to IBD. However, I started to realize in early 2000 that all of the growth funds were loading up with the same stocks (Cisco, Sun Microsystems, Dell, and other tech and Internet stocks). I felt like we owned a few stocks rather than mutual funds. Because of this and because of IBD, we went to cash in March of 2000.

We have both retired early since then because we did not lose so much like most folks did. Thank you, IBD. You are our success.

Jim Musial: I am a fairly new investor and only into my second year as an IBD subscriber. My "professional" money manager has not protected my portfolio very well over the past 18 months, losing upwards of 40 percent in my mutual funds. However, my personal "learning" portfolio is doing well at a 6 percent gain for the same time frame. The reason I'm in the "green" is clearly due to adhering to the IBD way. I think the "New America" section provides a wealth of potential candidates to study on a daily basis and it is where I've found my two gems.

If I can pick winners in a bear market, anyone can. I'm ready to take matters in my own hands. Best regards (and thanks, IBD).

Alan Terence Kahn: December 2000 I bought shares of Engineered Support Systems after reviewing the chart and bio of the company in your business publication. This was the first stock I ever bought. To make a long story short, I sold EASI at $53 a share in November 2001 after buying it at $22.10. My profit . . . was 125 percent. This was something I had never done before. The dramatic change in its Accumulation/Distribution tipped me off to sell into the rally.

You have opened up a brave, new world for me and I am very grateful, as my intention is to accumulate approximately $10 million in the next 15 years. I have a ways to go, but IBD will assist me. Once again, many thanks.

Mark Rothenberg: After reading *How to Make Money in Stocks* and reading IBD on a daily basis, I finally put all the pieces to the investing puzzle together, and found out it's not a puzzle at all. Just stick to the philosophies and rules as they have been laid out, and successful investing will follow. I am hoping it will make for earlier retirement!

Bennet Simonton: Your paper is a great improvement over the *Wall Street Journal*, which I have read for years. WSJ just doesn't have what an investor needs. Your articles about companies are very useful.

Lee Smith: *Investor's Business Daily* is the only financial publication that is a successful tool for investing. I have learned more from it than I have learned in 10 years as a stockbroker.

Jon E. Bassett: I became familiar with IBD only recently and wish I had known of this outstanding investors' publication at the outset! Since I have begun taking advantage of what IBD has to offer, my successful trades have multiplied significantly! Thanks for an extremely useful and interesting paper! Please continue doing the outstanding job I have come to expect from your expert staff . . . and pass on to them my gratitude for a job well done!

J.R. Hobbs: When I was looking at my accounts this year . . . I was astonished at how well I had done versus the S&P. It takes discipline to keep up with the market . . . and I have never found anything that helped me like your newspaper and Web site have.

Alan Terence Kahn: None of my successes would have occurred if I had not read IBD. Most assuredly, I would have bought blindly and held on blindly without the expertise available to the public through IBD.

I recommend your newspaper to everyone I meet. More investors need to become acquainted with IBD. Many thanks for your assistance.

John Moyers: I cannot tell you how helpful your publication has been to me. In 1995, while pursuing my M.D. and Ph.D. degrees, I took a night job at UPS, and saved every dime. I was nearly dead from overwork. Finally, I began reading *Fortune* and one day I picked up your publication. I was mesmerized. Less than one year later, I was a first-generation millionaire; your publication gave me 90 percent of the tips I used and pointed me to half of the remaining 10 percent. I cannot thank you enough for your publication; it is truly a work of genius.

Marilyn Ellis: I saw Bill O'Neil on CNBC in the late '80s and tracked his market calls, and he was accurate! An eye opener! In learning Mr. O'Neil's CAN SLIM method, my husband and I have been able to retire early and build the house of our dreams, and look forward to years of travel in Europe . . . a life we never dreamed we could achieve before we had IBD in our lives. We have now happily become accustomed to annual 100 percent returns in our portfolio in up markets and appreciate being safely on the sidelines in the bear markets. Thank you!

Joey Wilson: Thank you so much for your service, as the change in my life is beyond what I ever imagined. I have enough cash to last me the rest of my life at age 52. When the working world dumped me due to my affliction, I found "y'all." Thanks are not enough, but it's all I have to offer and to tell folks the word you pass on. Thanks for my life back.

Fred Benedetto: I've been reading IBD since its inception. I started with $5000 and three years later, it escalated to $50,000. Why? Because of IBD. If you want to be on top of the stock market, the only tool is *Investor's Business Daily.* Need I say more?

APPENDIX E

A Loud Warning to the Wise About Bear Markets!!!

Let me offer one last bit of guidance. If you are new to the stock market or the historically tested and proven strategies outlined in this book, or, more important, if you are reading this book for the first time near the beginning or middle of a bear market, do not expect the presumed buy patterns to work. Most will definitely be defective. **You absolutely do not buy breakouts during a bear market.**

The price patterns will be too deep, wide, and loose in appearance compared to earlier patterns. They will be third- and fourth-stage bases; have wedging or loose, sloppy handles; have handles in the lower half of the base; or show narrow V formations moving straight up from the bottom of a base into new highs, without any handle forming. Some patterns may show laggard stocks with declining relative strength lines and price patterns with too much adverse volume activity or every week's price spread wide.

It isn't that bases, breakouts, or the method isn't working anymore; it's that the timing and the stocks are simply all wrong. The price and volume patterns are phony, faulty, and unsound. The general market is turning negative. It is selling time. Be patient, keep studying, and be 100 percent prepared. Later, at the least expected time, when all the news is terrible, winter will ultimately pass and a great new bull market will suddenly spring to life. The practical techniques and proven disciplines discussed here should work for you for many future economic cycles.

INDEX

AAII (American Association of Individual Investors), xiv–xv, 154
Accumulation, 3
Adobe Systems, 127
After-tax profit margin, 41
Alliance Semiconductors, 128
Amazon.com, 31, 80, 81
America Online, 42, 77, 78, 79, 82, 86, 128
America Power Conv., 128
American Can, 20
American dream, 139
American Machine & Foundry, 29, 75
American Research & Development, 55
AMF, 61
Amgen, 70, 73, 128
Annual earnings, 39, 148–149
AOL Time Warner, 31, 35, 37

Apollo (APOL), xv, 153
Apple Computer, 31, 124
Apple South, 128
Ascend Communications, 73, 128
Ascending base pattern, 67–68
Asset allocation, 111–113
AT&T, 28, 31
Atchison Topeka & Santa Fe Rail, 20
Averaging, 108–109

Bajkowski, John, xv, 141
Balanced funds, 115
Bar chart, example, xviii
Bear markets, 173
    cash, 100
    characteristics, 32
    follow-throughs, 11–12
    identifying, 8
    market direction, 145

Bear markets (*Cont.*):
  percentage corrections, 15–16
  saucer pattern, 58–59
  selling short, 100–102
Berlin Wall, 137
Bethlehem Steel, 94
Big-Cap Index Plus, 162
Biogen, 130
Blow-off top pattern, 82
Boeing, 66, 78
Bonds, 114–115
Boyd, Katie, 126
Broadcom, 103
Brock, Lou, 2
Brunswick Corp., 31, 54, 75
Buffet, Warren, xv
Bull markets
  cup with a handle pattern, 47, 69
  earnings per share, 42–43
  follow-throughs, 9–11
  identifying, 8
  market direction, 145
  market leaders, 11, 19
  PE ratios, 113–114
  pivot price, 69
  stock splits, 91–93
Bush administration, 132–139
Bush, George W. (President), 139
Business Objects, 130
Buying
  at bottom of bull market, 10
  on dips, 24
  increasing positions, 100
  mutual fund strategies, 22–23

Buying (*Cont.*):
  a put, 95
  rules, 39–46, 142–145
  strategies, 26–28
  timing of, xiii–xiv

California blue-chip utilities, 28
Call options, 95
Callaway Golf, 128
CAN SLIM™ Investment Research Tools
  annual earnings, 148–149
  approach, xv, xvi, 146–152
  earnings per share, 156
  identifying institutional sponsors, 158
  market direction, 152, 159
  performance, 151
  quarterly earnings, 155–156
  rules, 142–145
  screening results, 152–154
  supply and demand, 157
Capital gains, 138–140
Cash, 100
C-cor.net, 103
CEOs, photos on magazine covers, 93
Channel lines, 84–85
Charles Schwab, 42, 51, 81, 82–83, 84, 130
Charts. *See also* Patterns
  advantages, xvii
  alternatives to, 80, 82
  investors.com, 54
  market index topped, 6
  market leaders peaked, 7
  reading, xvii–xix

Charts (*Cont.*):
  tightness, 70
  types of, 46
Checkpoint Software, 130
Chrysler, 55
Circuit City Stores, 31, 127
Cisco Systems, 31, 32, 35, 36, 42,
  52, 57, 65, 90, 104, 128
Clinton, Bill (President), 139
Closed-end funds, 114
CMGI, 104
CNBC on MSN Money, 151
Cobra Golf, 129
Cold War, 137
Columbus, Christopher, 2
Commercial Bankshares, 153
Commissions, 116
Compaq Computer, 56, 127
Compuware, 102
Comverse Technology, 130
Corning, 31
Costco Wholesale, 121, 124, 127
Crown Cork & Seal, 75
Cup with a handle pattern,
  47–58, 68–69, 77, 119–121

Daily Graphs® service, 42, 88
Daily volume. *See also* Price
  abnormal, 68
  effect of professional invest-
    ing, 23
  high, 8
  tracking, 3–4
  uptrends, 2–3
Data Analysis holding company,
  xvi
Datagraph charts, 124

Deficit problem, 132–137
Dell Computer, 122, 129
Delta Air Lines, 59
Democrats, 139
"Deworseification", 94
Digital Switch, 129
Distribution, 3–4. *See also* Sell-
  ing
Diversification, 32, 97–98
Dividends, 114, 137–138
Double bottom pattern, 59–64,
  74, 123
Dow Jones Industrials
  1974 market bottom, 12
  1978 market bottom, 13
  1982 market bottom, 13
  1987 market top, 14
  compared to NASDAQ, ix
Downtrends, identifying, 4–8
Dreyfus, Jack, xiv
Duquesne Systems, 127
Duveen, Lord, 125

Earnings growth, 39, 126
Eastman Kodak, 31
eBay, 130
Economic cycles, 126
Economic indicators, 1–4
*e*IBD™, 54
EMC, 31, 106, 129
Emerson, Ralph Waldo, 11
Emulex, 70, 72, 127
Enron, xx
Entrepreneurial companies,
  156–157
EPS (earnings per share), 39,
  42–43, 126, 142, 156

Ericsson, 31
Ericsson, L.M., 29
Etek Dynamics, 130
eToys, 94

Fairchild Camera and Instrument, 77–78, 79
False rallies, 9
FAO Schwarz, 31
Fidelity Funds, 94
Fidelity Investments, xiv
Flat base pattern, 64–66
Flexibility, 11
Follow-throughs, 9–12
Ford Motor, 31, 127
Foreign stocks, 112, 115
Fourth-stage bases, 87
Franklin Research, 127
FTI Consulting (FCN), xv, 153

Gains, offsetting losses, 27
Game Technology (IGT), xv
Gap, 31
Gartner, 87
Genentech, 127
General Electric, 20, 29, 31
General Motors, 94
Gillette, 127
Glenayre Technologies, 61
"Good" stocks, 18
"Good-buy money," 24
Goodyear Tire & Rubber, 31
Grand Central Station, 94
Greenspan, Alan, 135
Gulf + Western, 94

Hedging, 33, 95, 97–98, 112
Helix Technology, 65
Home Depot, 31, 42, 53, 70, 72, 91, 127
Hubbard, Glenn, 126

IBM Corporation, 12
Indexes. See Market indexes
Individual investors. See also Portfolio management
  accepting reality, 96–97
  advantages, 15–16, 23
  testimonials, 163–172
Industrial stocks, 20
Industry groups, 43–45, 91, 102–108, 144
Innovators, 20–21
Institutional investors
  identifying, 144, 151–152, 158
  low profile of, 22
  role in determining market direction, 21–22
  stocks held, 45
Intel, 31
International Game Technology, 42, 122, 124, 129, 153
Investment myths, 12, 14–15, 32, 97–98
Investors. See Corporate investors; Individual investors
Investor's Business Daily
  1992 market distribution system picks, 15
  2002 Economic Conference, 126
  "Big Picture" column, 8, 16

Investor's Business Daily
    (*Cont.*):
  daily charts, 4
  EPS Rating, 39, 42
  "Friday Weekly Review" sec-
    tion, 43
  net gains of subscribers, xv
  RS ratings, 88–91
  tracking industry groups,
    43–45
Investors.com charts, 54
IPOs (initial public offerings),
    20–21, 126, 138–139
Iraqi crisis, 161–162

JC Penney, 31
JDS Uniphase, 31, 58, 92, 107
Johnson, Ned, xiv
JP Morgan Chase, 31

Kennedy administration,
    135–136
Kerr McGee Oil, 75
King World, 127
Kmart, 31
Kohl's, 91, 129

Laidlaw Transportation, 127
Lefevre, Edwin, xiv
Levitz Furniture, 71
Limit orders, 113
Limited Brands, 89, 120
Limited Stores, 127
Ling, Jimmy, 94
Ling-Temco-Vought, 94
Liquidity, 116
Livermore, Jesse, 33, 77

Liz Claiborne, 42, 127
Loeb, Gerald, xiv, 32–33
Long-term investors, 28, 99–100,
    138. *See also* Portfolio man-
    agement
Losses, 25–26, 27
Low-priced stocks, 110–111
Lucent Technologies, 29, 30, 105
Lynch, Peter, xv, 94

Marion Labs, 128
Market averages, 2–3
Market bubble, ix, xiii, 18–19,
    23–24, 134, 139
Market cycle, 76
Market direction, 21–22, 145,
    152, 159
Market history, 77
Market indexes, 4, 6, 9
Market leaders. *See also* Portfo-
    lio management
  in bull market, 11, 19
  channel lines, 84–85
  characteristics, 46
  cycles, 127–131
  identifying, 150–151, 157–159
  peaked, 7
Market performance, 18
Market recovery, 1929 market
    leaders, 20
Market technicians, 2
Marketability, 110
Markets
  consistency, 11
  downtrends, 4–8
  rallies, 9–10
Mattel, 31

McDonald's, 31
Medical Care Int., 129
Merck, 42, 128
Mercury Finance, 129
Mergers and acquisitions, 94
Micro-cap stocks, 148
Micron Technology, 31, 70, 85, 129
Microsoft, 42, 129
Microstrategy, 50
Money market funds, 100
Monogram Industries, 66, 70
Morningstar.com, 151
MSN Money, 151
Mutual fund companies
  buying strategies, 22–23
  management policies, 15
  stock investments, 21

NASDAQ
  bottom-building process, 161–162
  compared to Dow Jones Industrials, ix
  distribution, 4
  March 2003 bottom, 10
Network Appliance, 57, 106, 130
New Stock Market Ideas, xvi, 164
New York Central Railroad, 20
Newbridge Networks, 129
Nextel Communications, 31
Nokia, 42, 51, 60, 89, 130
Novell, 128
NVR, 60

Oracle, 31, 62, 70, 123, 124, 130
Oshkosh Truck Corporation, 153

Pan Am building, 94
Patterns
  ascending base, 64, 67–68
  blow-off top, 82
  cup with a handle, 47–58, 68–69, 74, 77, 119–121
  double bottom, 59–64, 74, 123
  flat base, 64
  identifying, 70, 74
  saucer, 58–59
  supply and demand, 74, 143, 149, 157
Paychex, 52
PE (price-to-earnings) ratio, 21, 78–79, 113–114, 155–156
Peoplesoft, 129
Pic 'N Save, 42
Pivot price, 69
PMC-Sierra, 130
Polaroid, 31
Portfolio management. See also Stocks
  asset allocation, 111–113
  balanced funds, 115
  bonds, 114–115
  cheap stocks, 109–110
  closed-end funds, 114
  commissions, 116
  dividends, 114
  foreign stocks, 112, 115
  industry groups, 43–45, 91, 102–108, 144
  key to success, 97
  liquidity, 116
  losses, 113
  PE ratios, 113–114
  selecting stocks, 118

Portfolio management (*Cont.*):
    stocks held, 98–102
    taxes, 117
    theories, 117–118
Price. *See also* Buying; Daily volume; Patterns; Selling
    drop of 50 or 60 percent, 24–25
    effect of professional investing, 23
    market averages, 2–3
    new highs in, 143
    patterns, 173
    per share, 110–111
    spread between high and low, 8
Price Co, 42, 123, 124–125, 128
Price scale, xviii
Professional investors, 22
Profit vs. loss ratio, 26
Pullback
    ascending base pattern, 64
    bottom point of handle, 69
    saucer pattern, 58–59
    temporary, 85

QLogic, 42, 53, 130
Qualcomm, 31, 35, 38, 82, 92, 131
Qualitative factors, 149
Quarterly earnings, 146–148, 155–156

Railroads, 20
Rationalization, 33
RCA (Radio Corporation of America), 19, 20

Reagan administration, 135, 136
Recessions, 132
Redman Industries, 67, 78
Reebok, 48–49, 128
Republicans, 139
RF Micro Devices, 131
Rite Aid, 31
ROE (return on equity), 41, 149
RS (relative strength), 88–91, 150

S&P 500
    1998 market bottom, 13
    1998 market top, 14
    AAII research, xv
    distribution, 4
"Safe" stocks, 18
Sales growth, 41
Saucer pattern, 58–59
SDL Inc, 131
Sea Containers, 119, 120
Sears Roebuck, 20
Sears Tower, 94
Selling
    3–to-1 profit-vs.-loss ratio, 26
    in bear markets, 100–102
    goals, 17–18
    mistakes, 75–76
    by professional investors, 23
    strategies, 26–28, 34
    taking profits, 5, 76, 102
    timing of, xiii
Service Merchandise, 29
Short selling, 100–102
Siebel Systems, 131
Simmonds Precision, 67, 70

Small business creation plan, 138–139
Social Security system, xi
Southern Pacific, 20
Sprint Fon Group, 31
St. Jude Medical, 129
Stalling action, 3. *See also* Distribution
Standard Oil, 20
Stock Investor Pro, 146, 147, 152
Stocks. *See also* Buying; Daily volume; Market leaders; Patterns; PE; Portfolio management; Price; Selling
annual earnings, 39, 148–149
assessing potential of, 118–125
average decline after peaks, 18
averaging, 108–109
avoiding catastrophic losses, 25–26
CAN SLIM characteristics, 45
chart bases, 85–88
cheap, 109–110
correction, 68–70
cutting losses, 109
dividends, 114
exposure to commitment, 27
foreign, 112
former leaders, 31–32
industry group, 43–45, 91
institutional sponsors, 45
IPOs, 20–21
liquidity, 116
marketability, 110

Stocks (*Cont.*):
merger and acquisition binges, 94
performance indicators, 68
pullbacks, 58–59, 64, 69, 85
qualitative factors, 149
quarterly earnings, 146–148
relative strength, 88–91, 156
screening systems, 153–154
selecting, 118
stock splits, 91–93
supply and demand, 74, 143, 149
warning signs, 83–84, 94
Sun Microsystems, 25, 31, 109, 131
"Super trend," 164
Supply and demand patterns, 74, 143, 149, 157
Surgical Care Affiliates, 129
Syntex, 119

Taxes, 117
TCBY (This Can't Be Yogurt), 42, 121, 124, 128
Technology companies, earnings per share, 41
Tellabs, 32, 129
Testimonials, 163–172
Teva Pharmaceutical (TEVA), xv, 153
Texas Instruments, 32
The Limited, 42, 124
Thiokol Chemical, 71
Three Com, 129
3M (Minnesota Mining & Manufacturing), 29

3–to-1 profit-vs.-loss ratio, 26
Tommy Hilfiger, 32
Tsai, Jerry, xiv
Tulip bulb mania, ix–x
Turner, Ted, 125
TXU Corp., 28, 31
Tyco International, 32, 63

UAL, 32
Uniphase, 131
United Healthcare, 130
Uptrending market, 3
U.S. Health Care, 129
US Steel, 20
Utilities, 20, 28

Value Line, number-one-ranked
    stocks, xvi
Verisign, 105

Veritas Software, 62, 131
Vitesse Semi, 131
Volume. *See* Daily volume

Wal-Mart Stores, 40, 43–45, 56,
    93, 128
Walt Disney, 32
Walton, Sam, 93
Watson Pharmaceuticals,
    63
Wedging up, 69
Whipsaws, 12
William O'Neil + Co., xvi
WONDA® service, xvi
WorldCom, xii, 32

Xerox, 29, 32

Yahoo!, xii, 24, 32, 107, 130